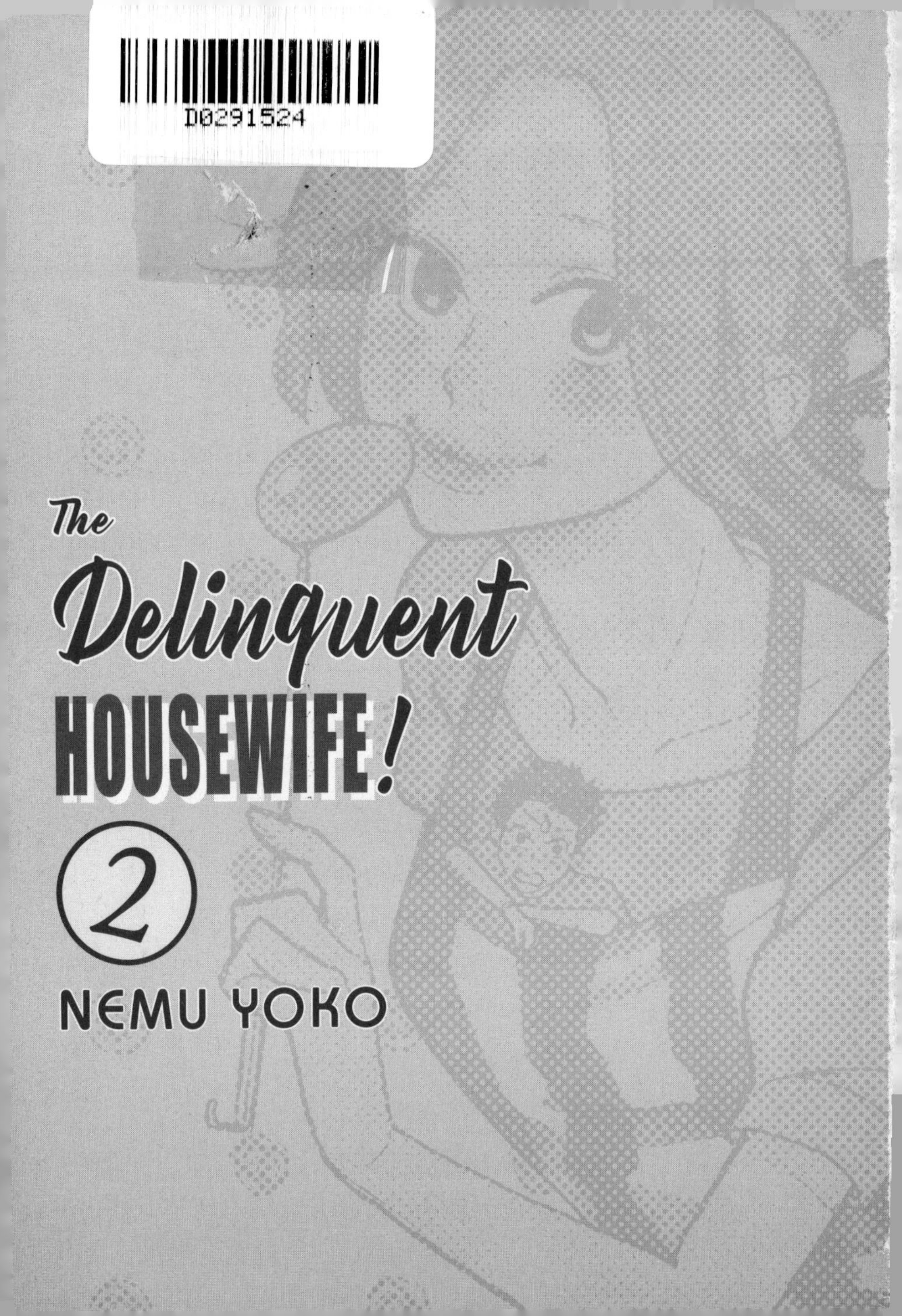

The Delinquent HOUSEWIFE!

2

NEMU YOKO

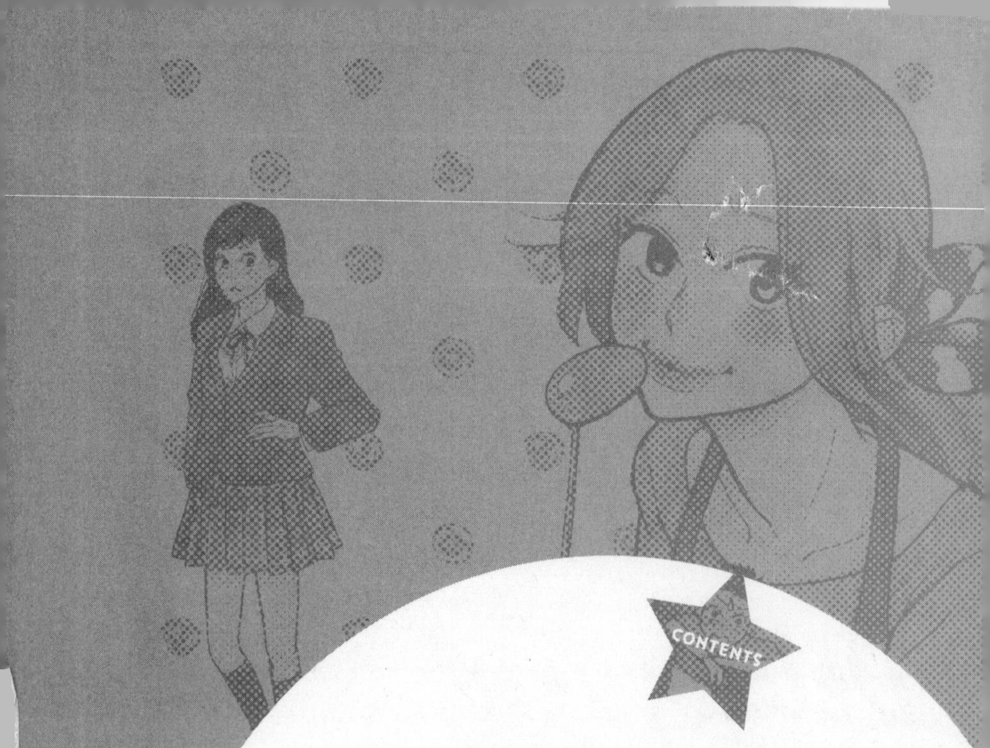

CONTENTS

9 SQUEAKY HAMMER TIME, PLEASE!

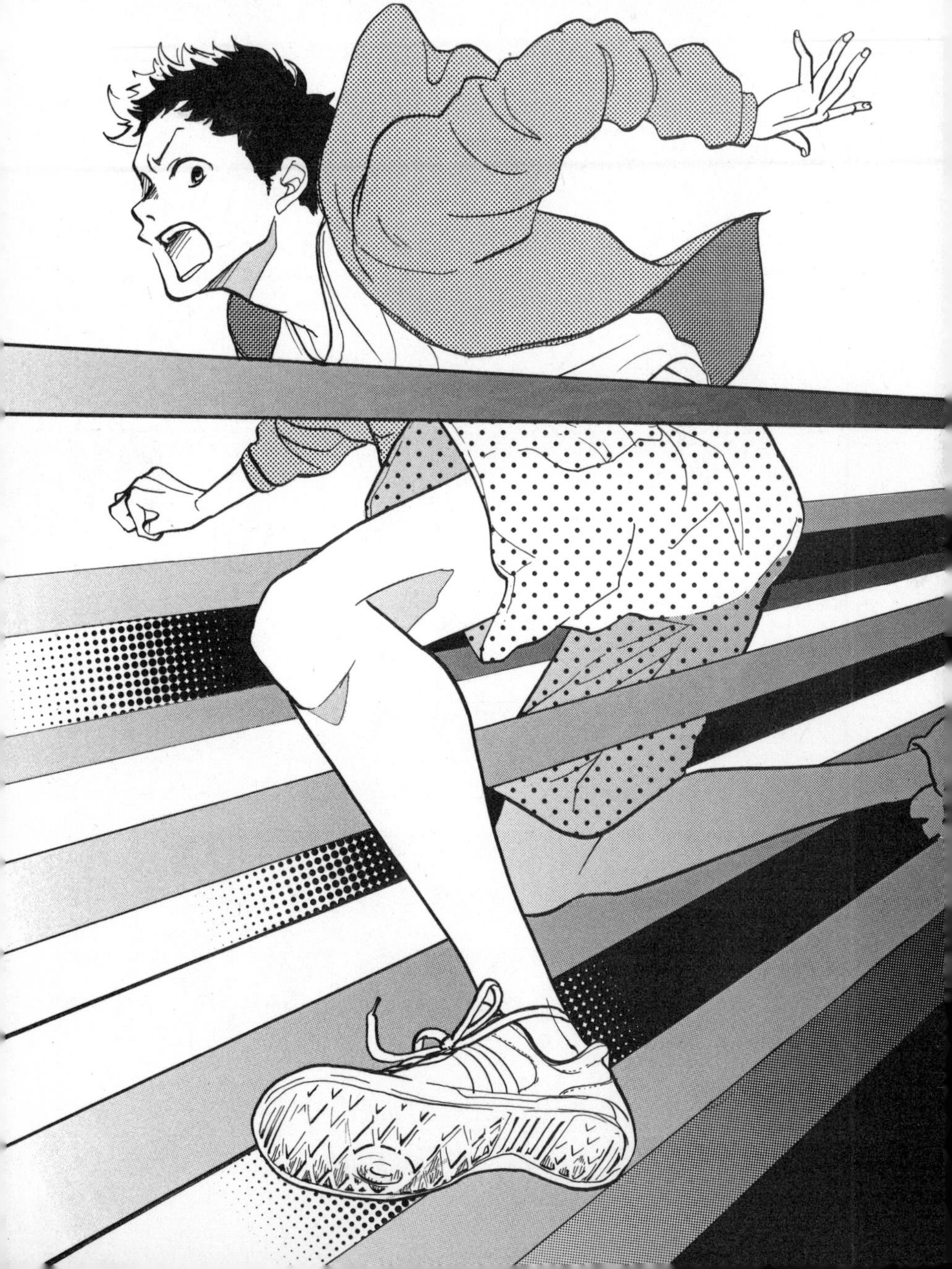

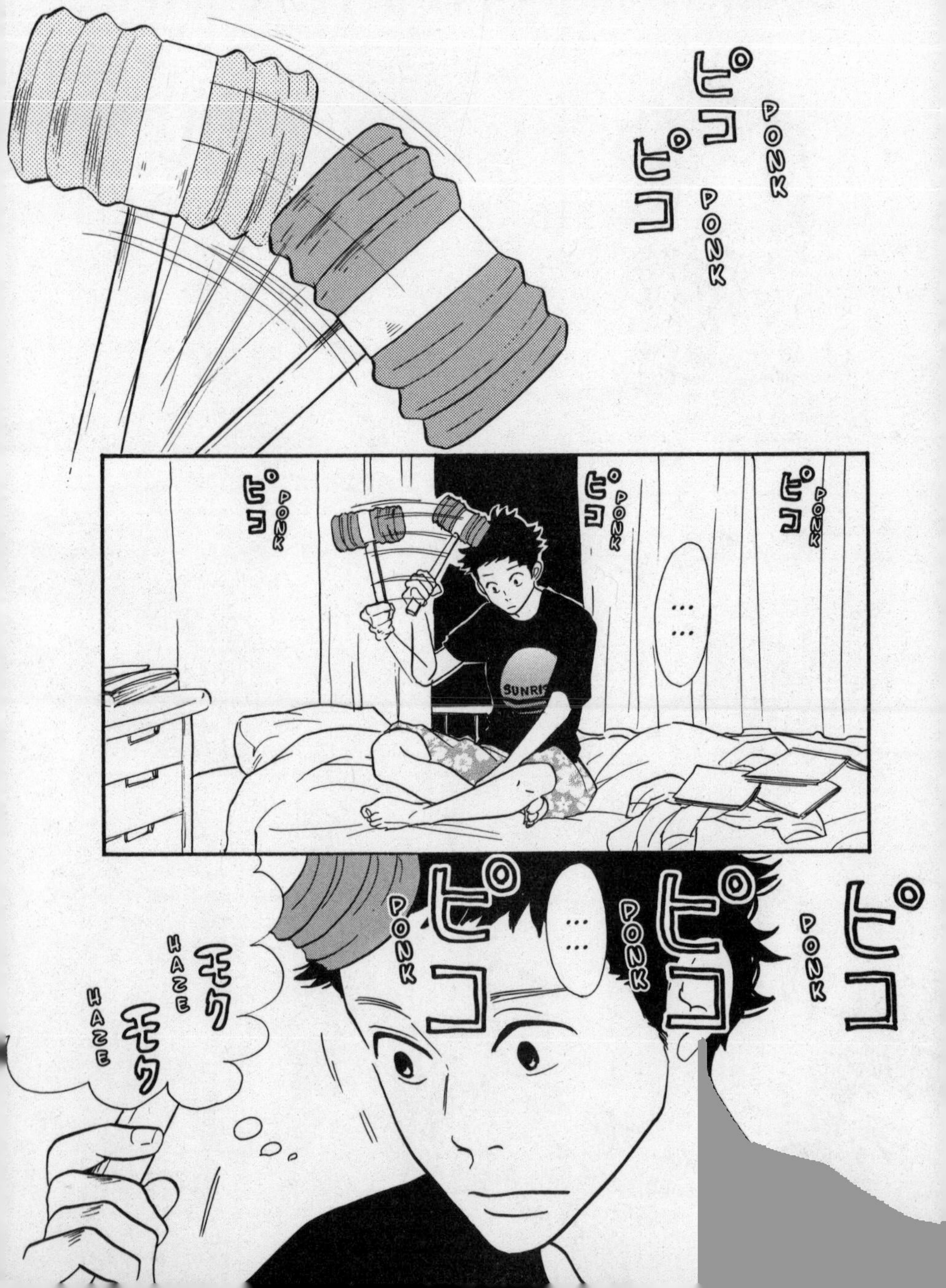

ピコ PONK
ピコ PONK
ピコ PONK
……
ピコ PONK
ピコ PONK
ピコ PONK
ピコ PONK
ピコ PONK
……
モク HAZE
モク HAZE

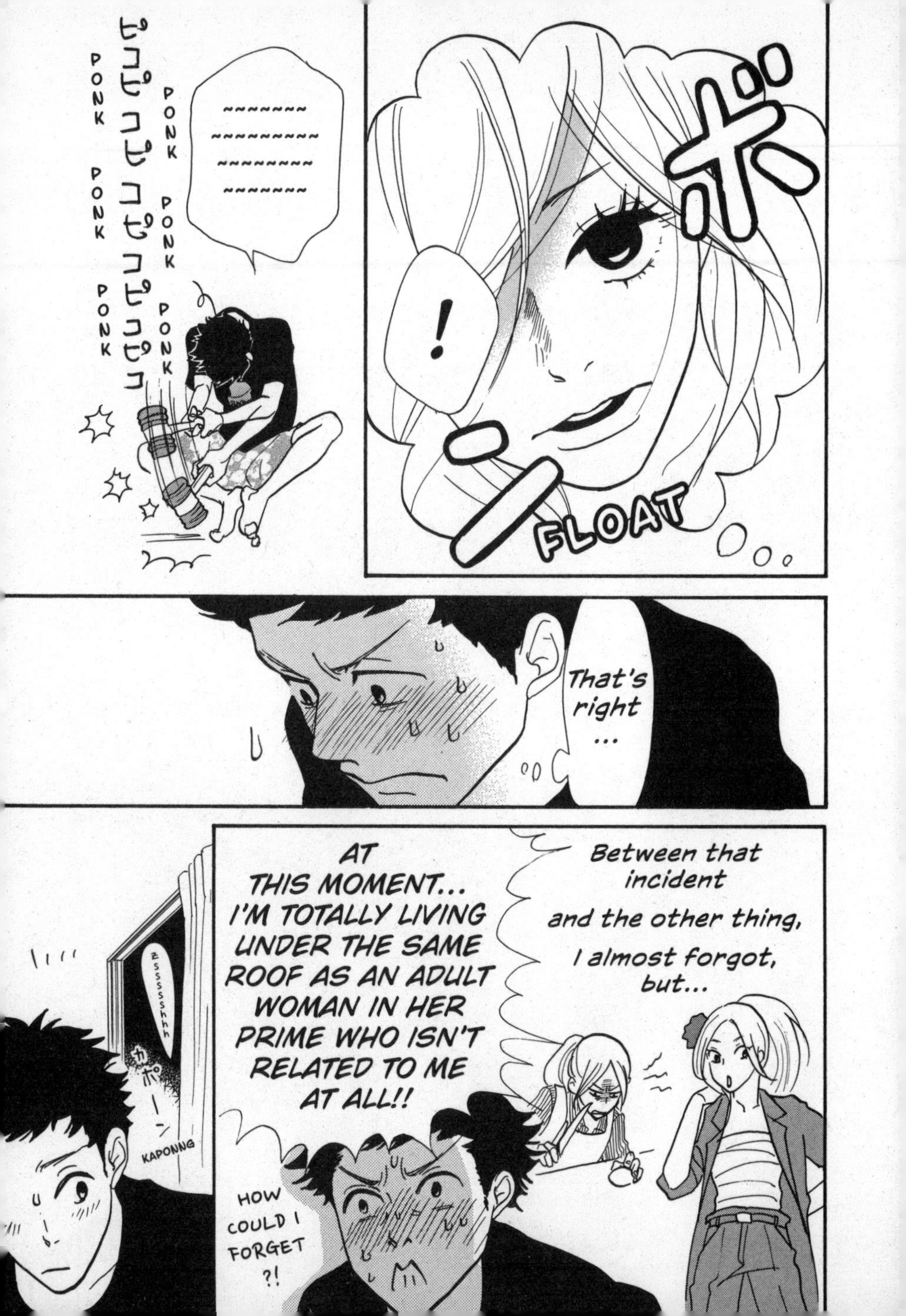

ボ
!
FLOAT
ピコピコピコピコピコピコ
PONK PONK PONK
PONK PONK PONK
That's right...
Between that incident and the other thing, I almost forgot, but...
AT THIS MOMENT... I'M TOTALLY LIVING UNDER THE SAME ROOF AS AN ADULT WOMAN IN HER PRIME WHO ISN'T RELATED TO ME AT ALL!!
HOW COULD I FORGET?!
カポーン
KAPONNG
zsssssshh

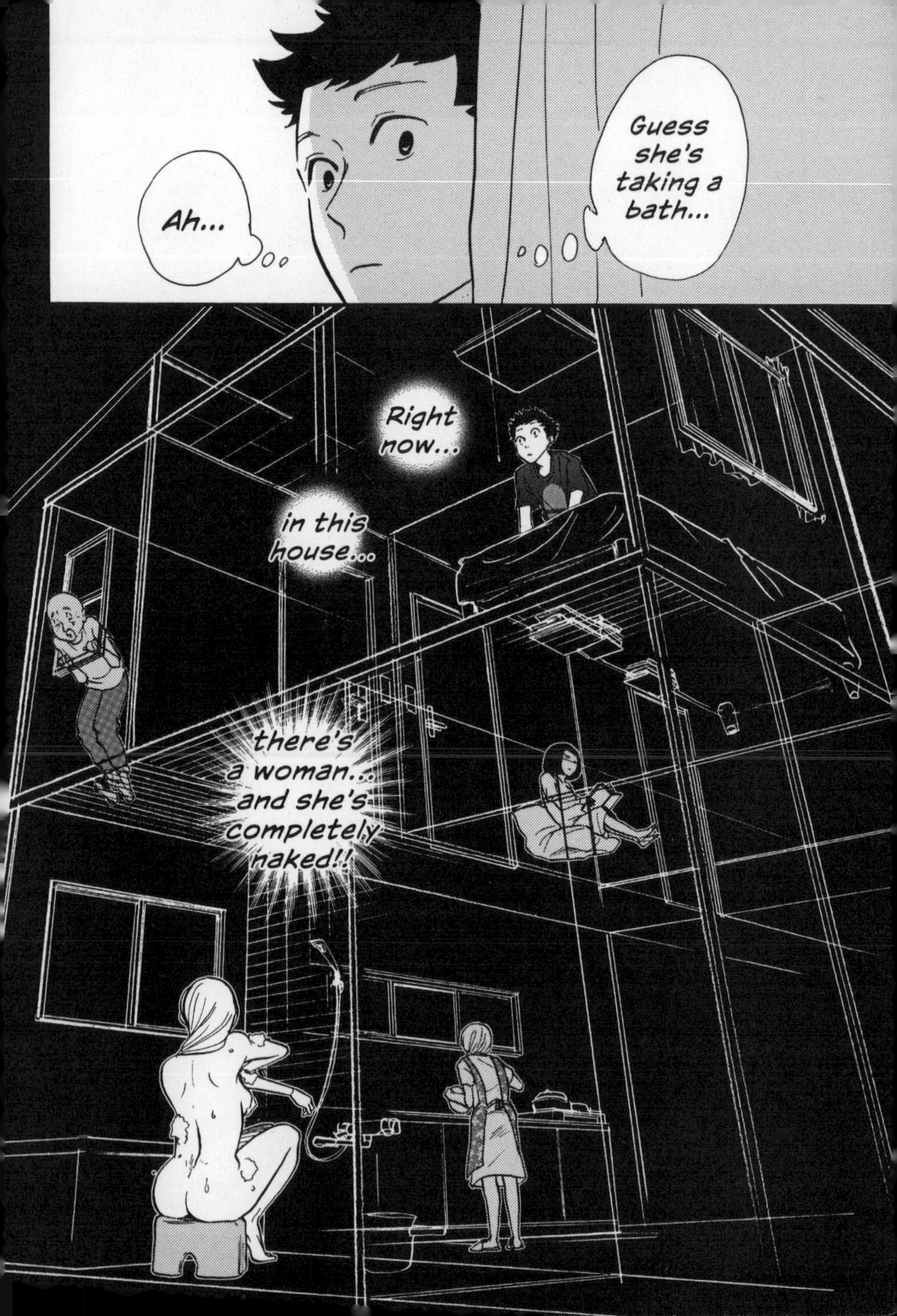
Guess she's taking a bath...
Ah...
Right now...
in this house...
there's a woman... and she's completely naked!!

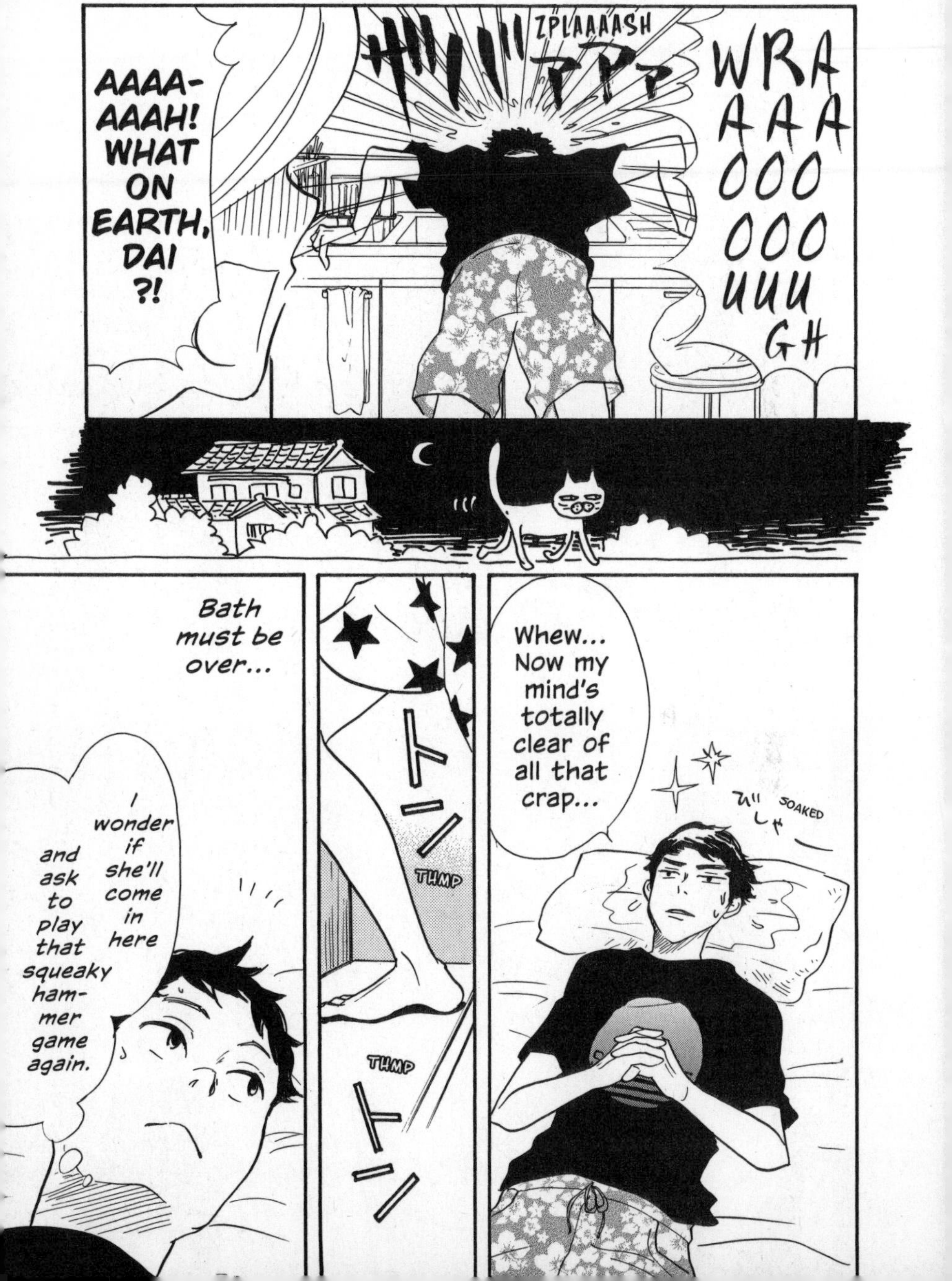
WRAAAAOOOOOOUUUGH
ZPLAAAASH
AAAA-AAAH! WHAT ON EARTH, DAI?!
Whew... Now my mind's totally clear of all that crap...
SOAKED
THMP
THMP
Bath must be over...
I wonder if she'll come in here and ask to play that squeaky hammer game again.

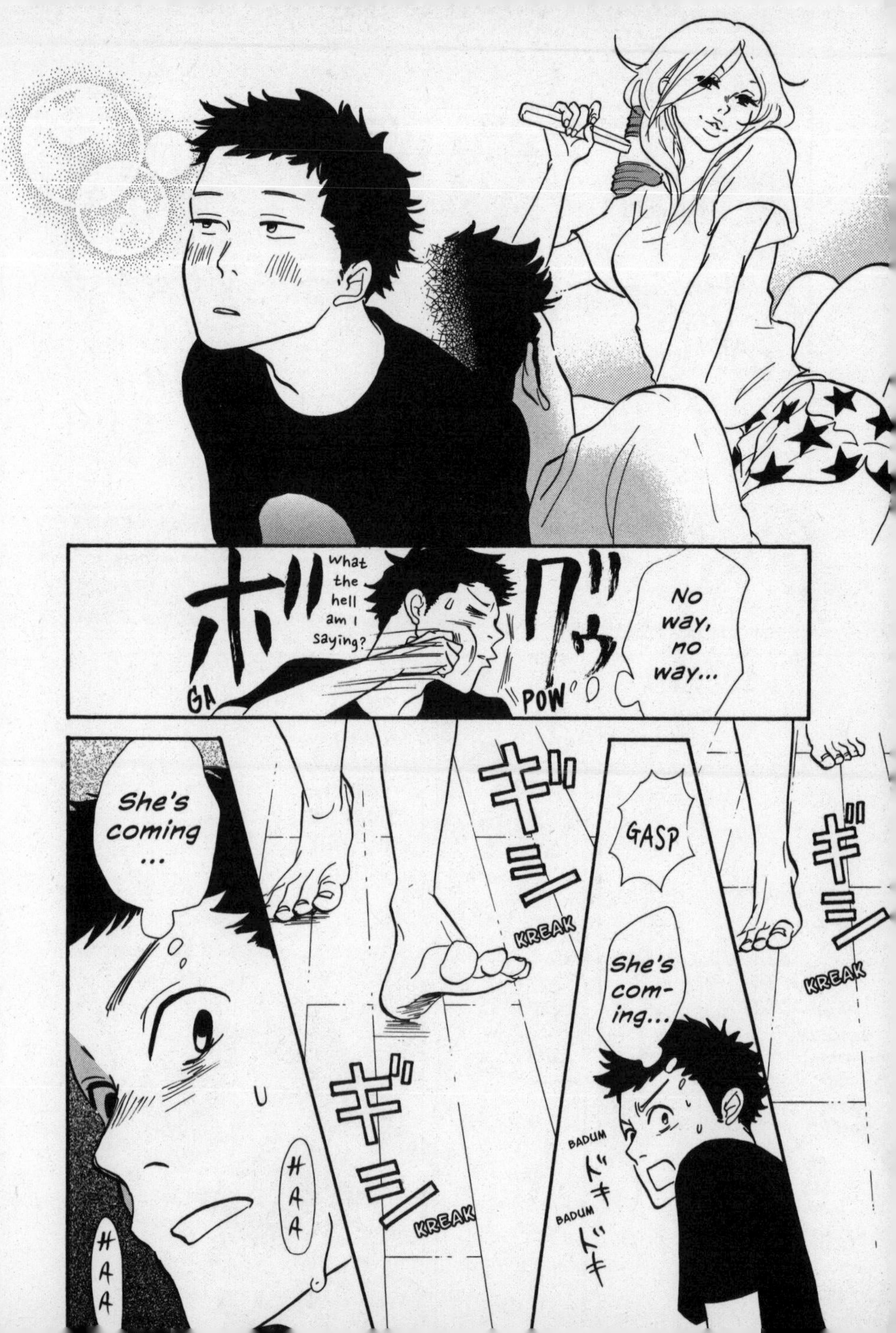
No way, no way...
POW
What the hell am I saying?
GA
KREAK
GASP
She's coming...
BADUM
BADUM
KREAK
KREAK
She's coming...
HAA
HAA

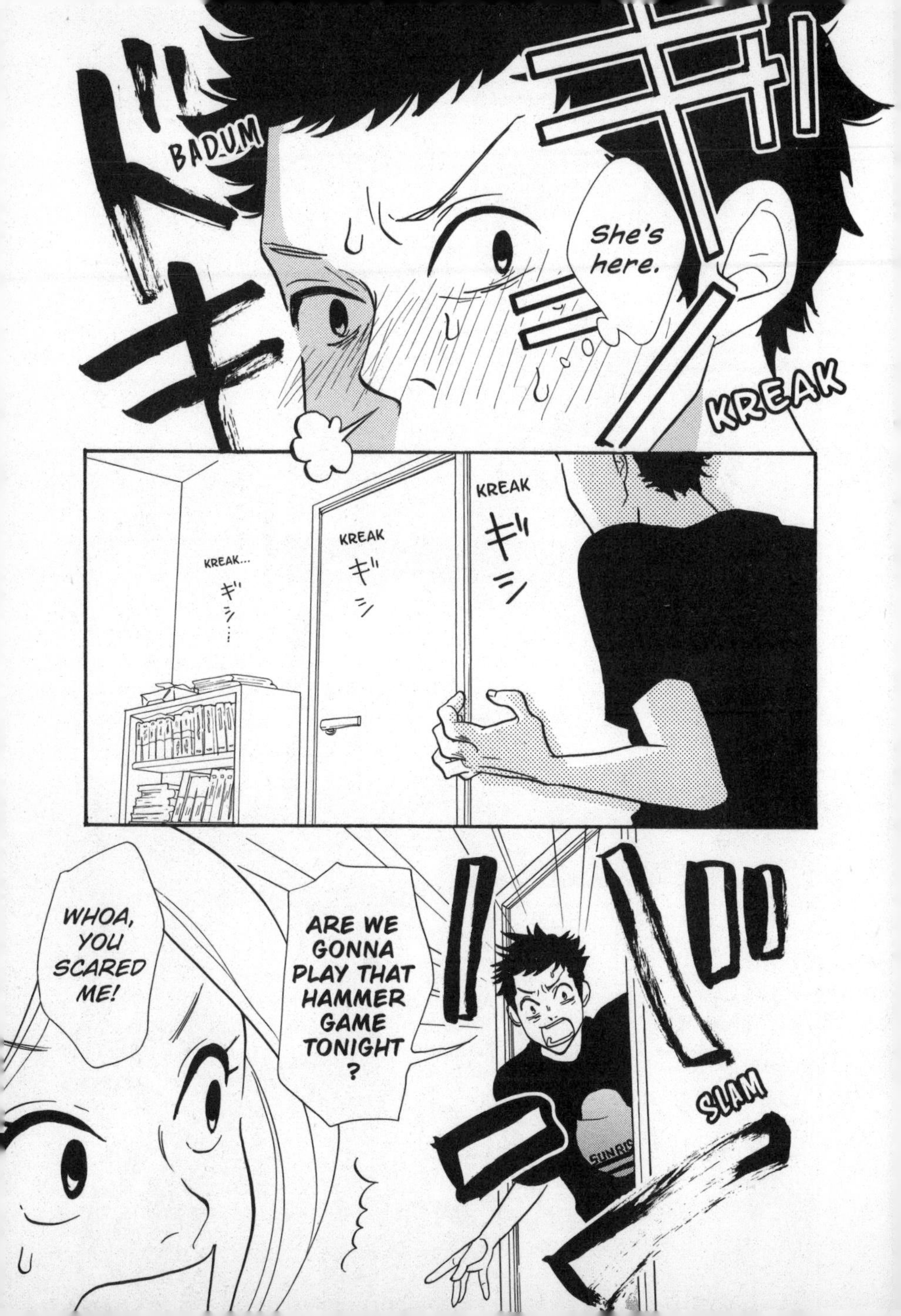

She's here.
BADUM
KREAK
KREAK
ギシ
KREAK
ギシ
KREAK...
ギシ...
SLAM
ARE WE GONNA PLAY THAT HAMMER GAME TONIGHT?
WHOA, YOU SCARED ME!

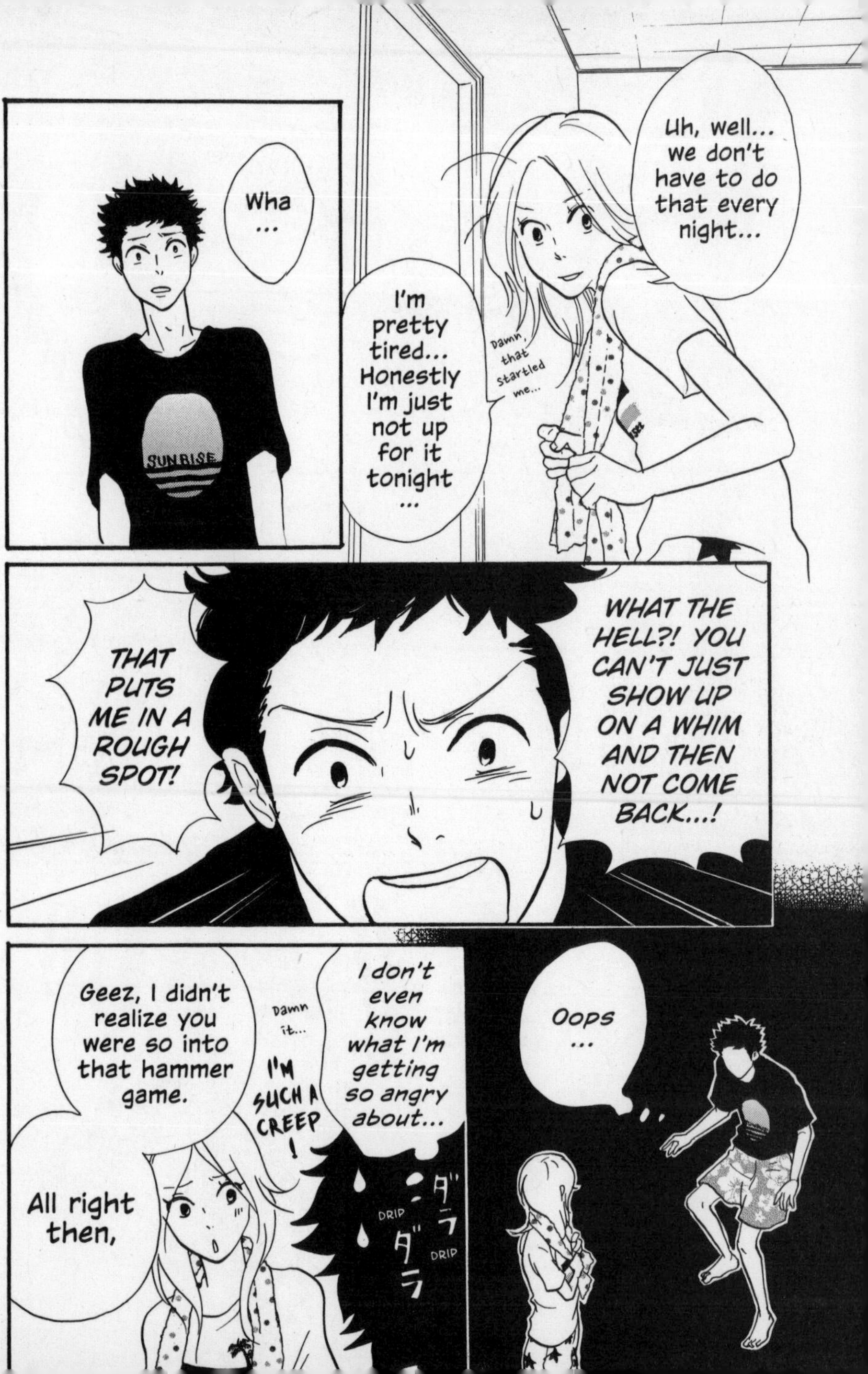
Uh, well... we don't have to do that every night...
I'm pretty tired... Honestly I'm just not up for it tonight ...
Damn, that Startled me...
Wha ...
WHAT THE HELL?! YOU CAN'T JUST SHOW UP ON A WHIM AND THEN NOT COME BACK...!
THAT PUTS ME IN A ROUGH SPOT!
Oops ...
I don't even know what I'm getting so angry about...
Damn it...
I'M SUCH A CREEP!
ダラ DRIP
ダラ DRIP
Geez, I didn't realize you were so into that hammer game.
All right then,

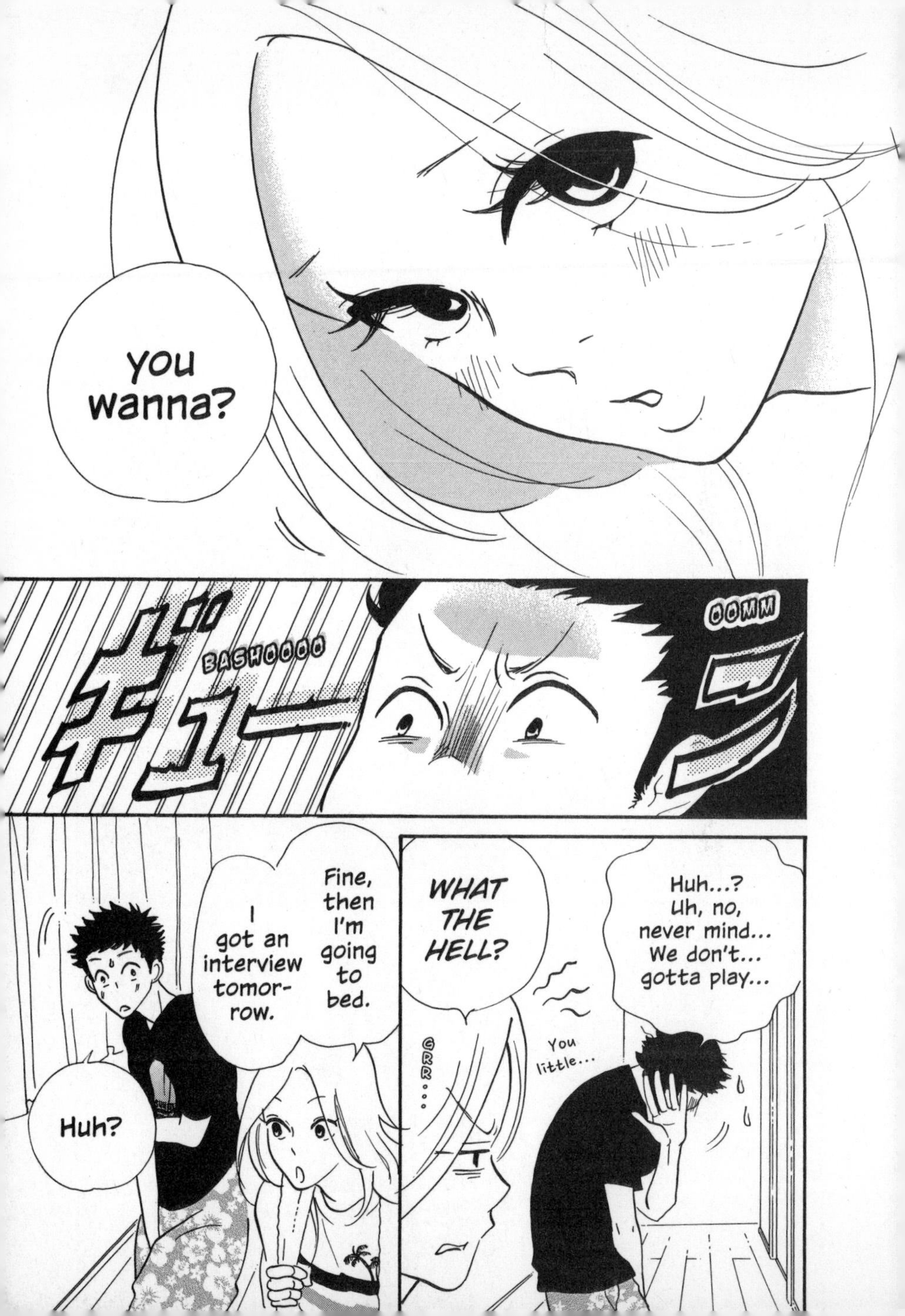
You wanna?
ギューン
BASHOOOOO
OOMM
Huh...? Uh, no, never mind... We don't... gotta play...
WHAT THE HELL?
You little...
GRR...
Fine, then I'm going to bed.
I got an interview tomor-row.
Huh?

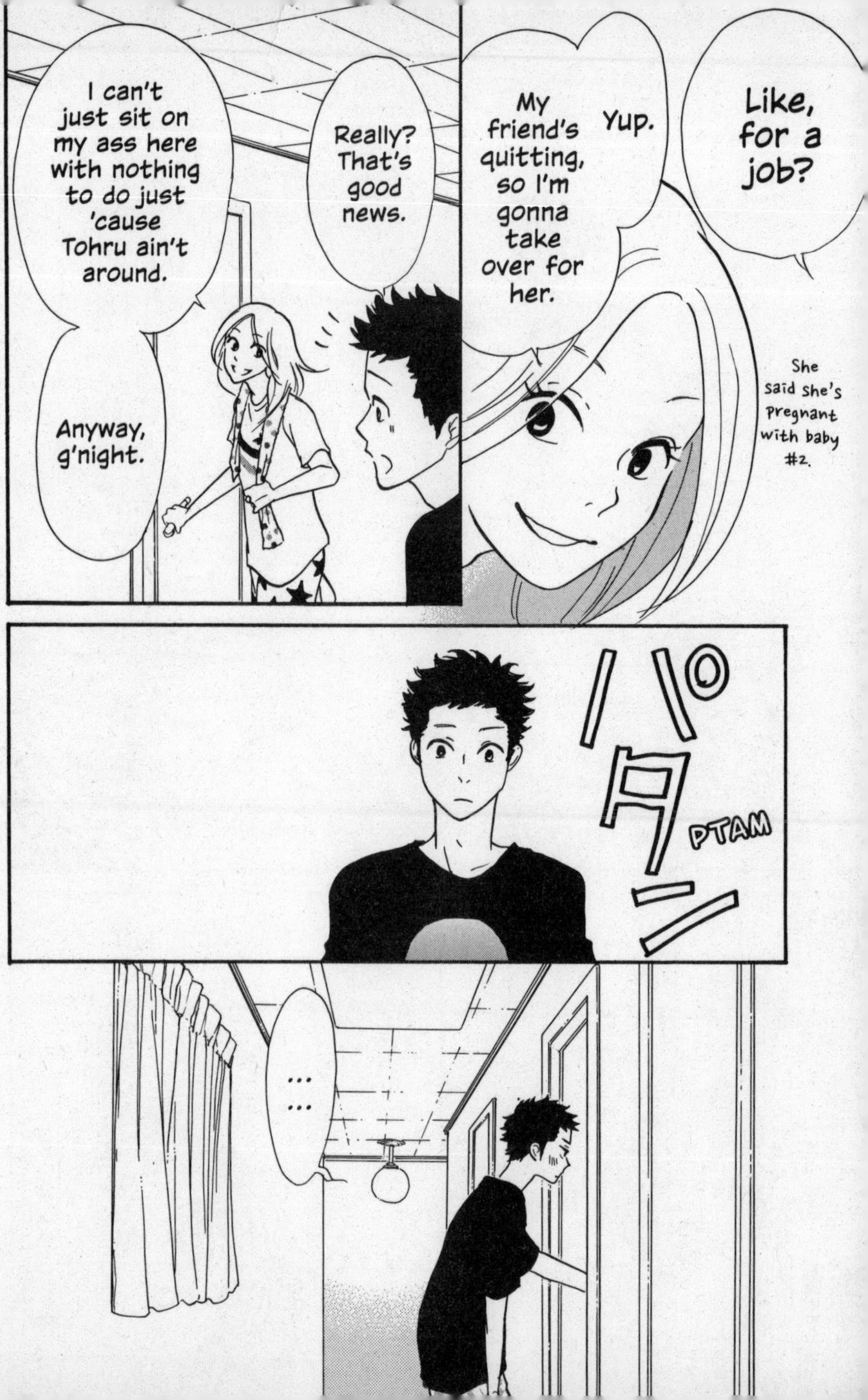
Like, for a job?
Yup.
My friend's quitting, so I'm gonna take over for her.
She said she's pregnant with baby #2.
Really? That's good news.
I can't just sit on my ass here with nothing to do just 'cause Tohru ain't around.
Anyway, g'night.
パタン
PTAM
......

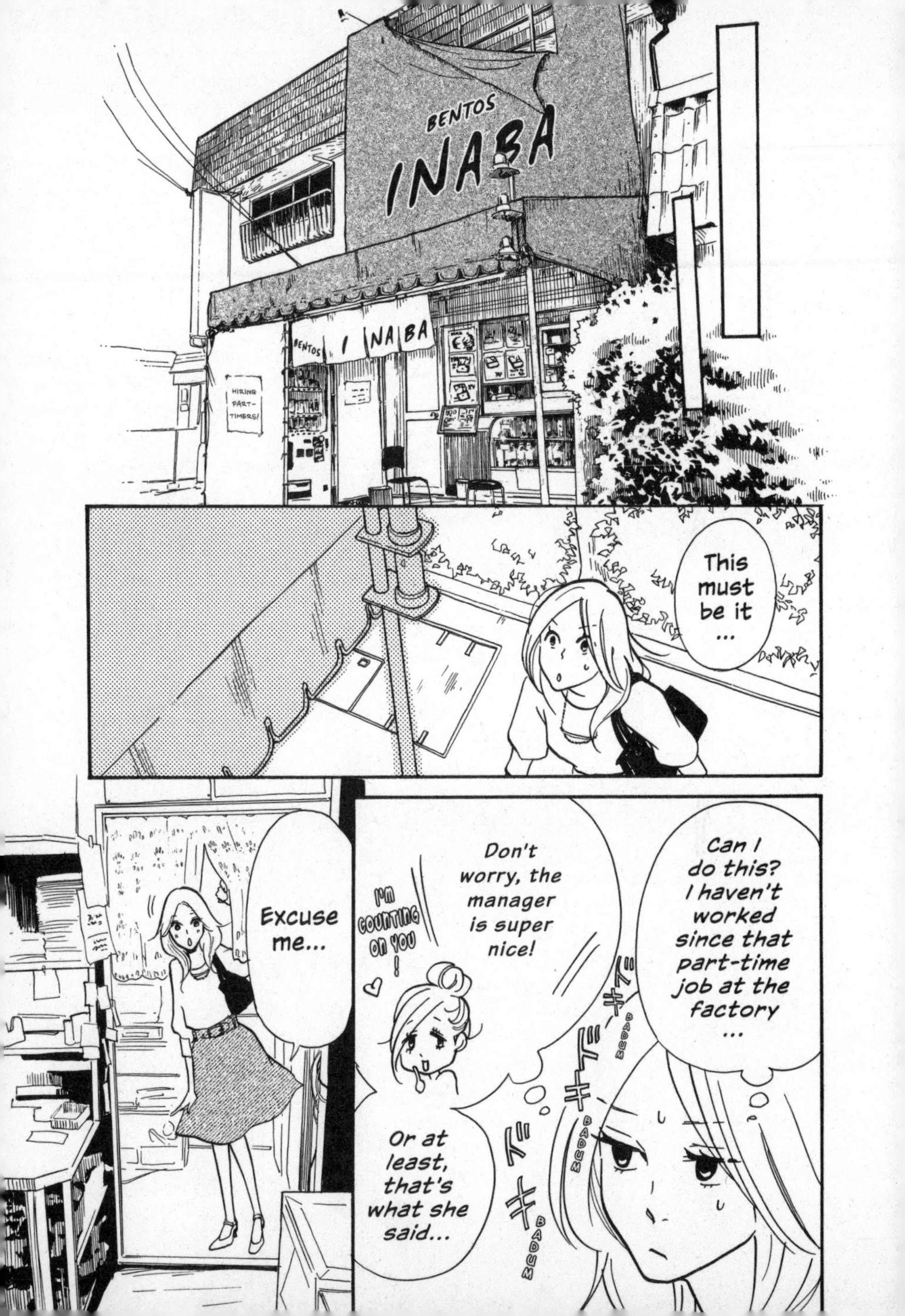
BENTOS
INABA
BENTOS I NA BA
HIRING PART-TIMERS!
This must be it ...
Can I do this? I haven't worked since that part-time job at the factory ...
BADUM
BADUM
BADUM
BADUM
Don't worry, the manager is super nice!
I'M COUNTING ON YOU!
Or at least, that's what she said...
Excuse me...

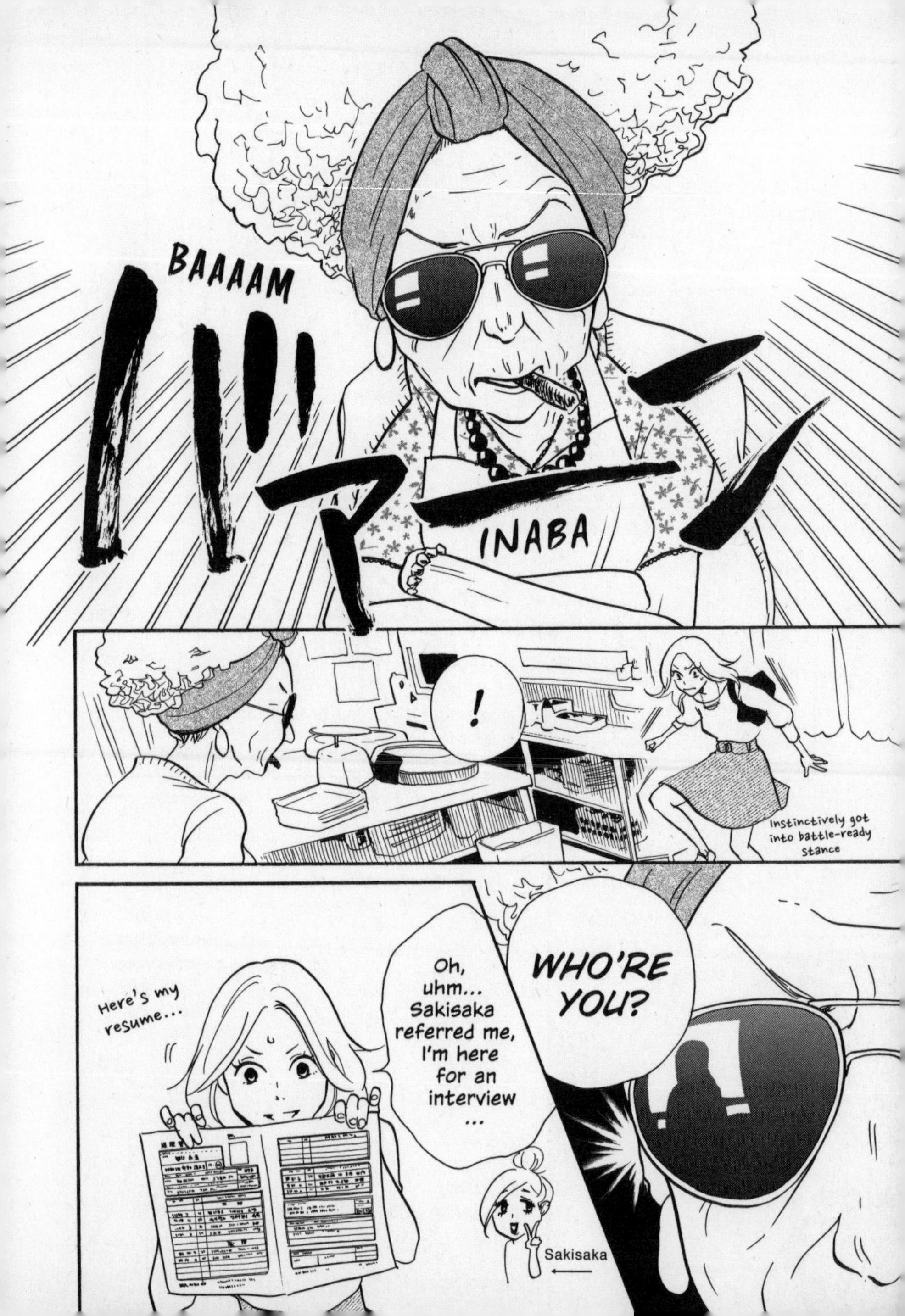
BAAAAM
バアーン
INABA
!
Instinctively got into battle-ready stance
WHO'RE YOU?
Oh, uhm... Sakisaka referred me, I'm here for an interview ...
Here's my resume...
Sakisaka

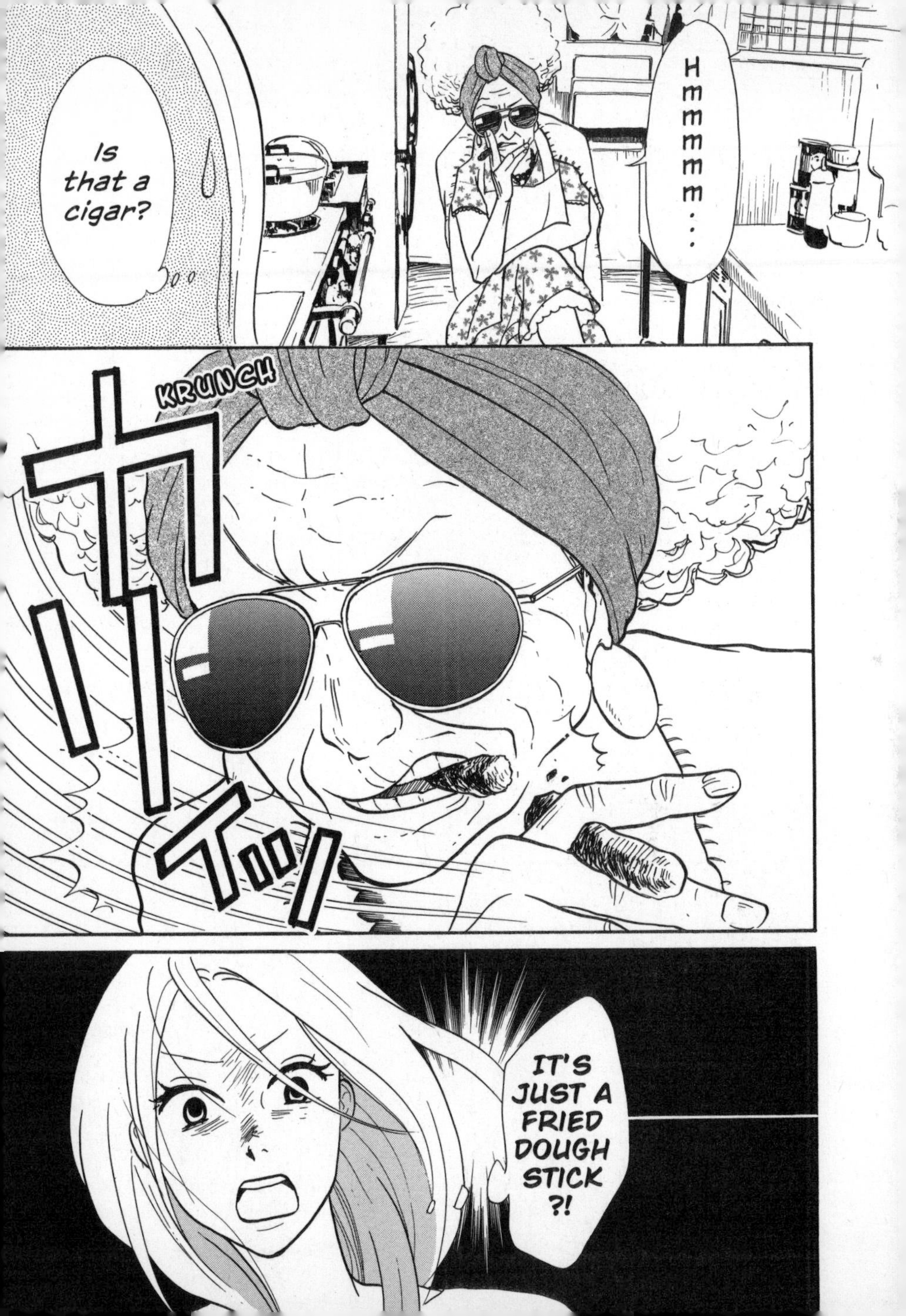
Hmmmmm...
Is that a cigar?
KRUNCH
IT'S JUST A FRIED DOUGH STICK?!

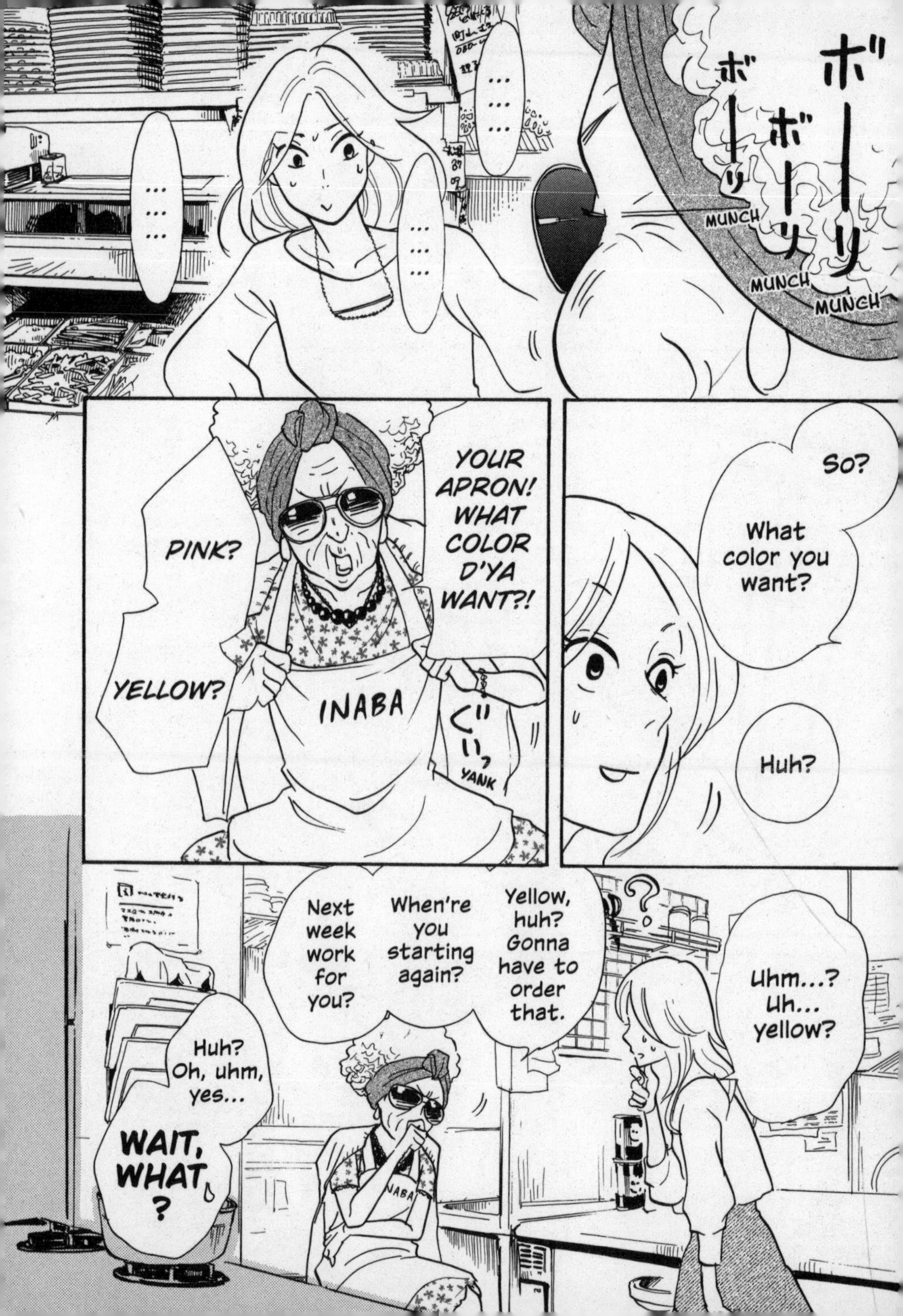

ボーリ
ボーリ
ボーリ
MUNCH
MUNCH
MUNCH
...
...
...
...
...
...
...
...
...
So?
What color you want?
Huh?
YOUR APRON! WHAT COLOR D'YA WANT?!
PINK?
YELLOW?
INABA
ぐいっ
YANK
Uhm...? Uh... yellow?
Yellow, huh? Gonna have to order that.
When're you starting again?
Next week work for you?
Huh? Oh, uhm, yes...
WAIT, WHAT?

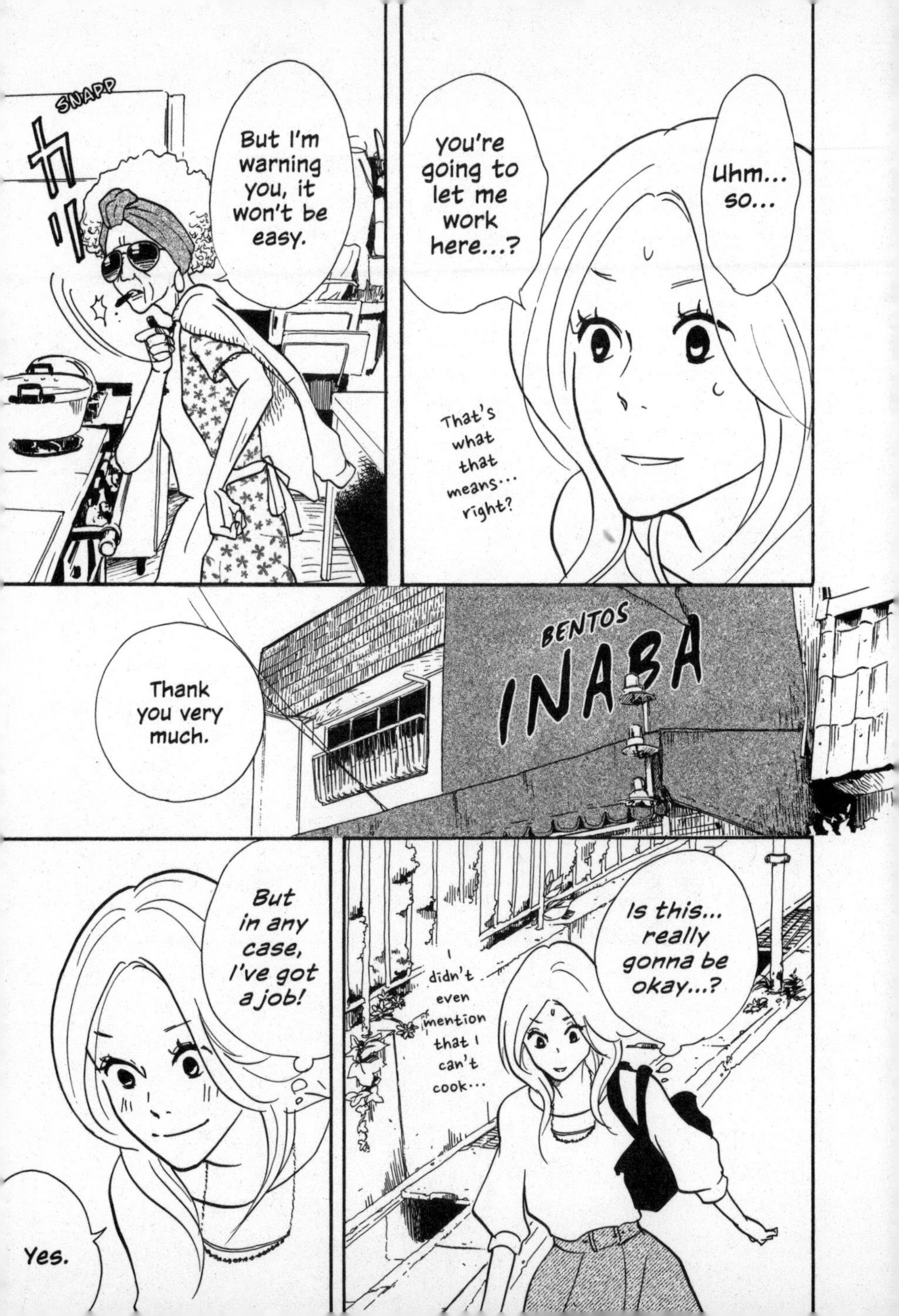
Uhm... so...
you're going to let me work here...?
That's what that means... right?
SNAPP
But I'm warning you, it won't be easy.
BENTOS
INABA
Thank you very much.
Is this... really gonna be okay...?
I didn't even mention that I can't cook...
But in any case, I've got a job!
Yes.

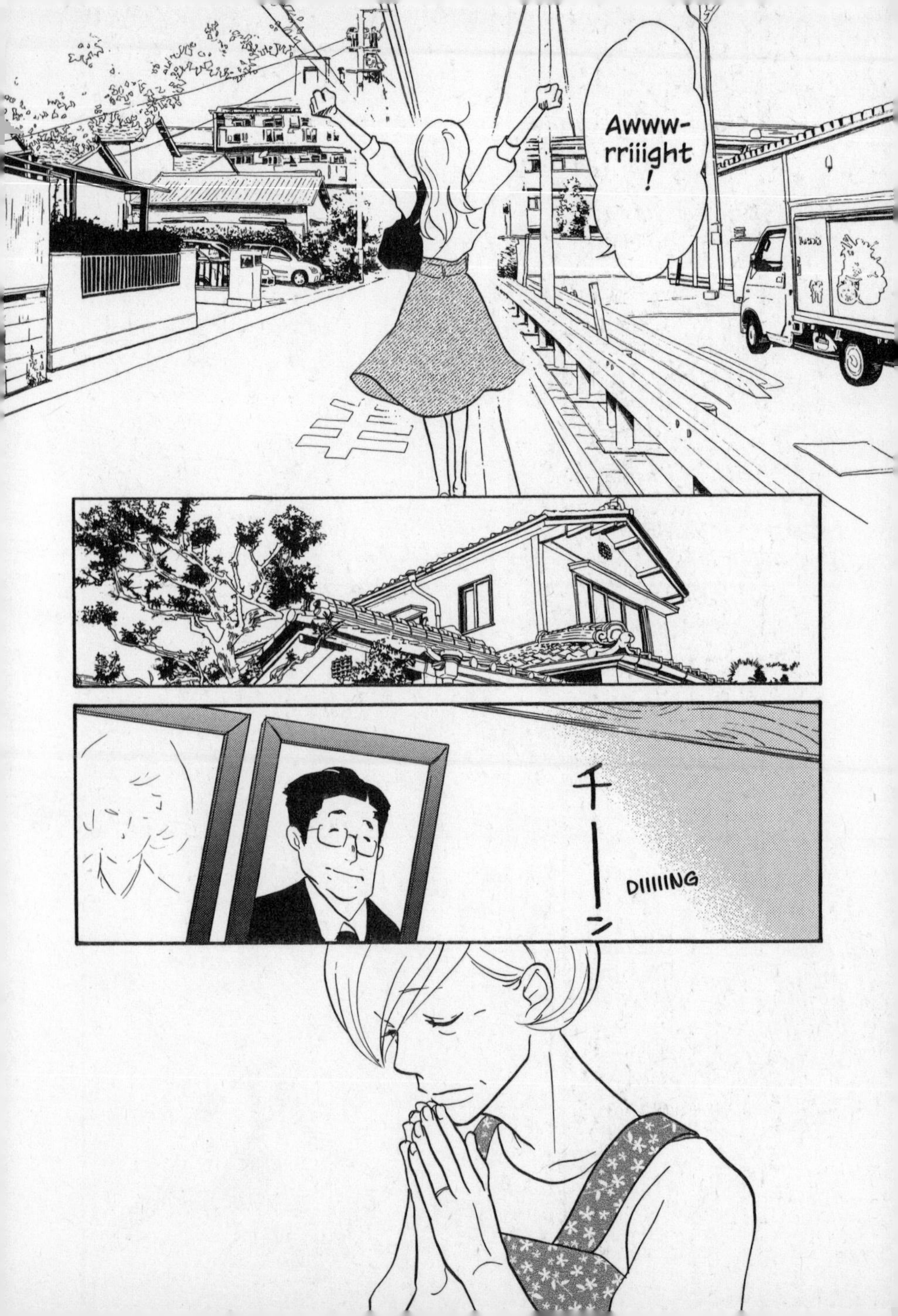
Awww-rriiiight!
チーン
DIIIIING

That was defi-nitely ...
a biker jacket.
LOVE
SORRY FOR BEING SO SEXY
Minoru, what should I do...
if Komugi really is a biker girl...

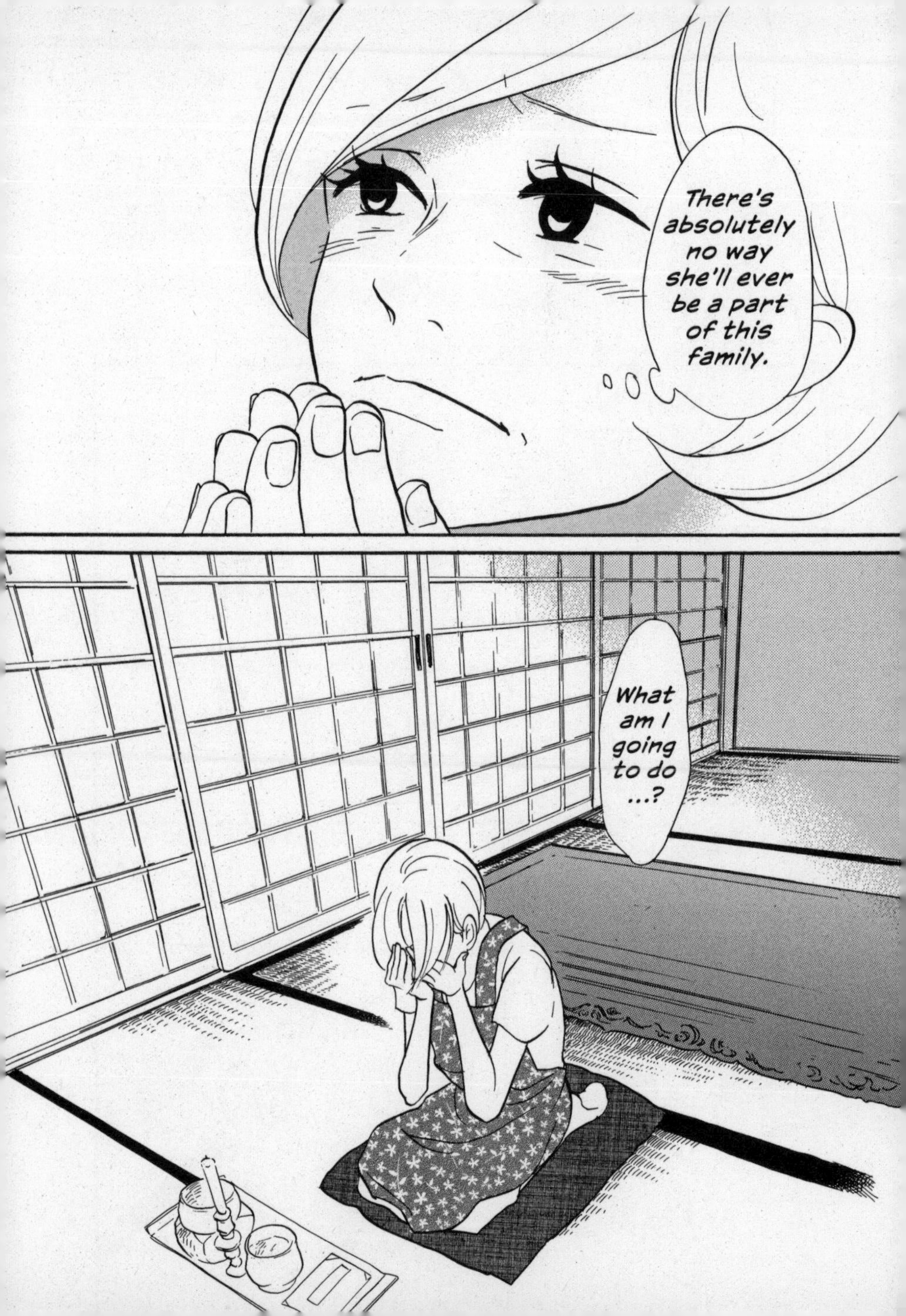
There's absolutely no way she'll ever be a part of this family.
What am I going to do ...?

10

THE SECRETS OF OTHERS

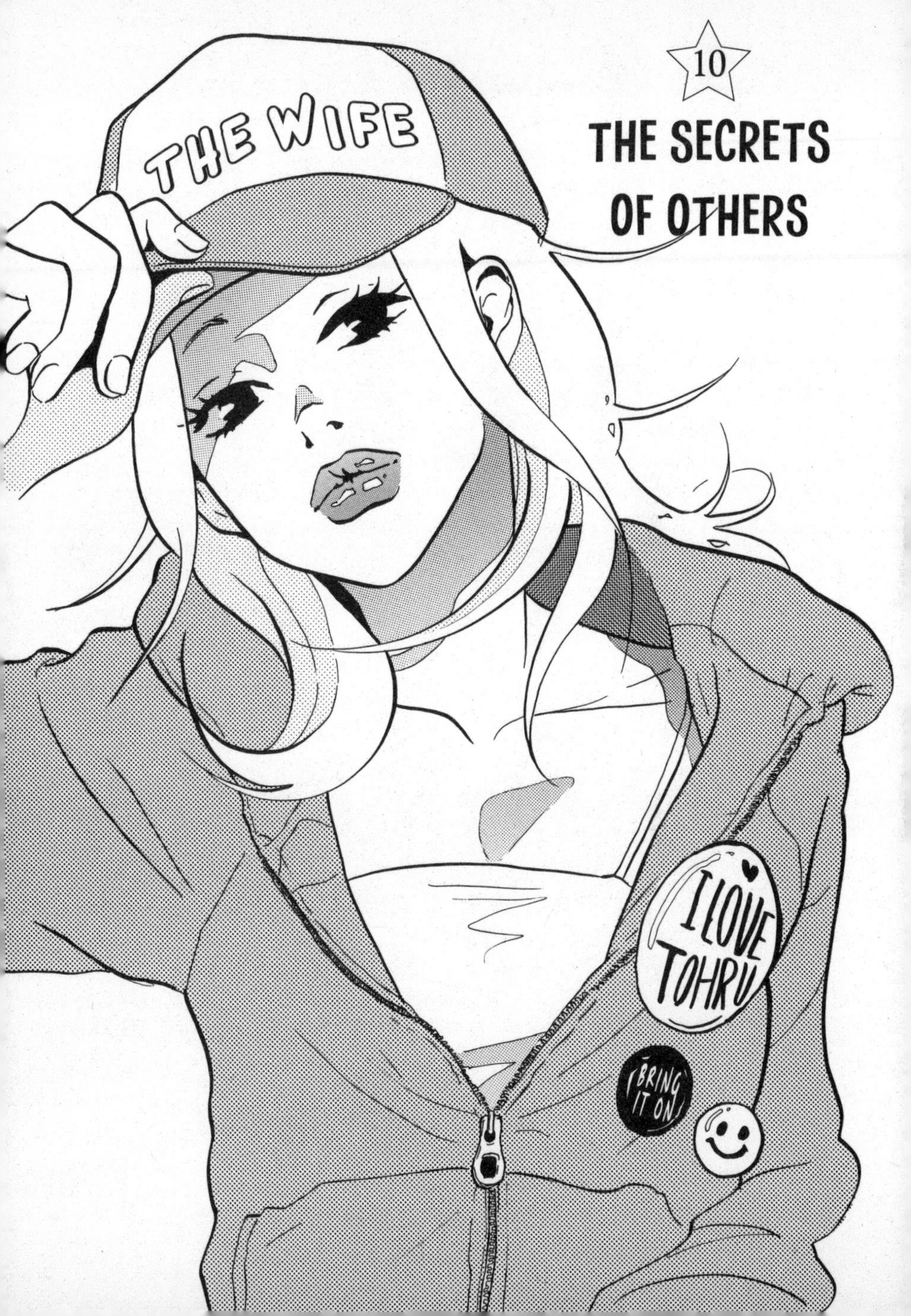
THE WIFE
I LOVE TOHRU
BRING IT ON!

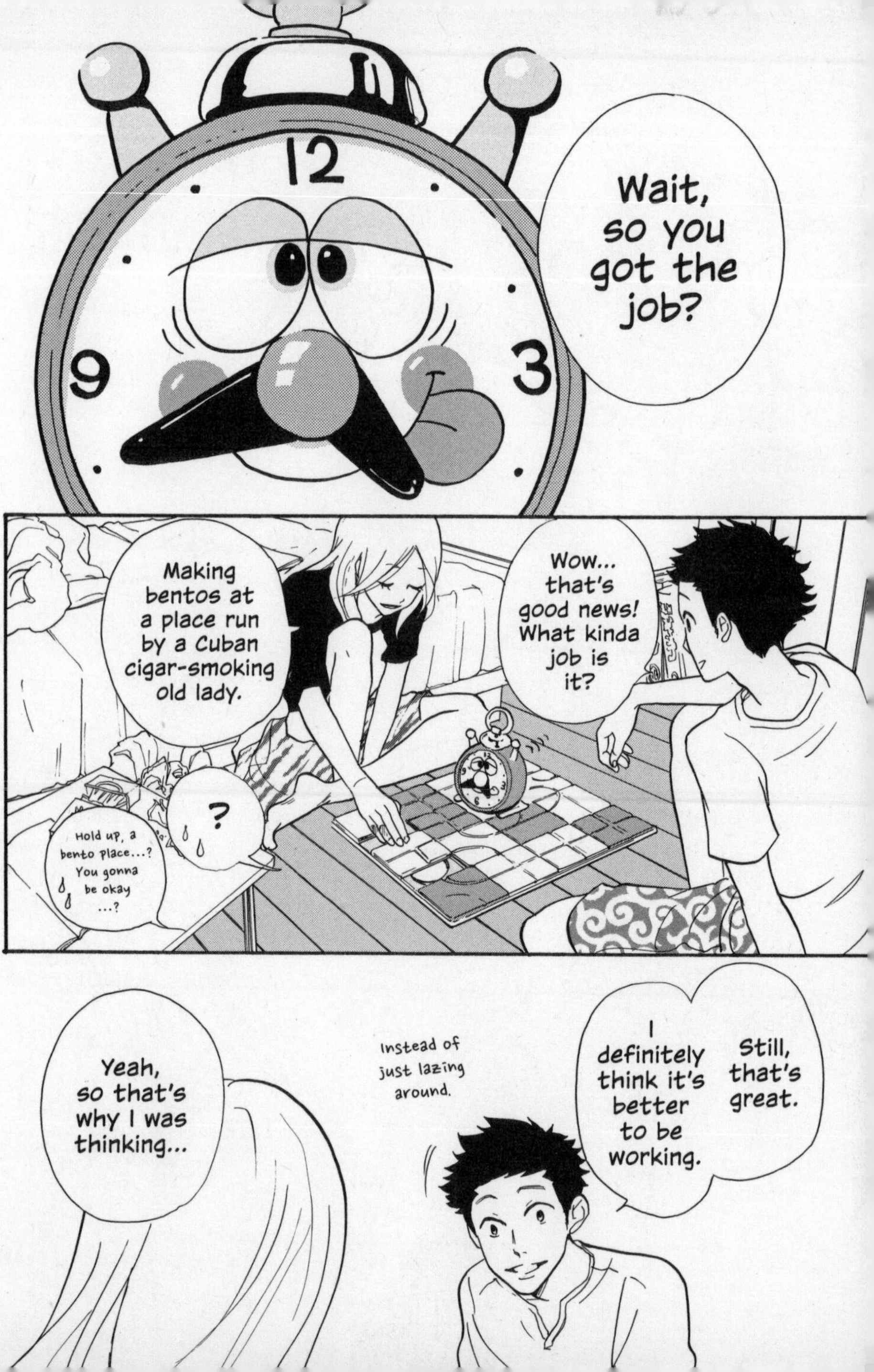
Wait, so you got the job?
Wow... that's good news! What kinda job is it?
Making bentos at a place run by a Cuban cigar-smoking old lady.
?
Hold up, a bento place...? You gonna be okay ...?
Still, that's great.
I definitely think it's better to be working.
Instead of just lazing around.
Yeah, so that's why I was thinking...

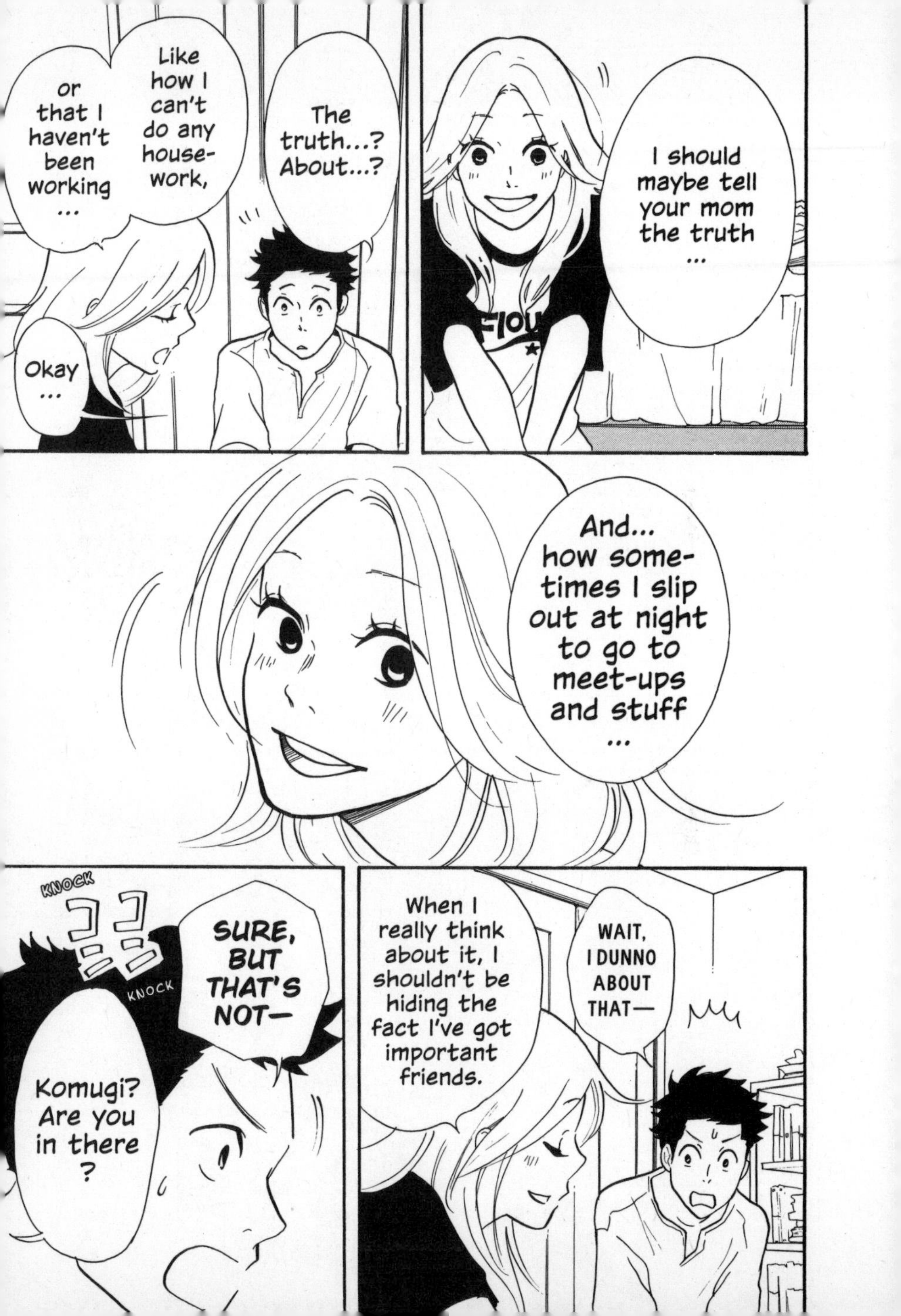
I should maybe tell your mom the truth ...
The truth...? About...?
Like how I can't do any house-work,
or that I haven't been working ...
Okay ...
And... how some-times I slip out at night to go to meet-ups and stuff ...
When I really think about it, I shouldn't be hiding the fact I've got important friends.
WAIT, I DUNNO ABOUT THAT—
SURE, BUT THAT'S NOT—
KNOCK
KNOCK
Komugi? Are you in there ?

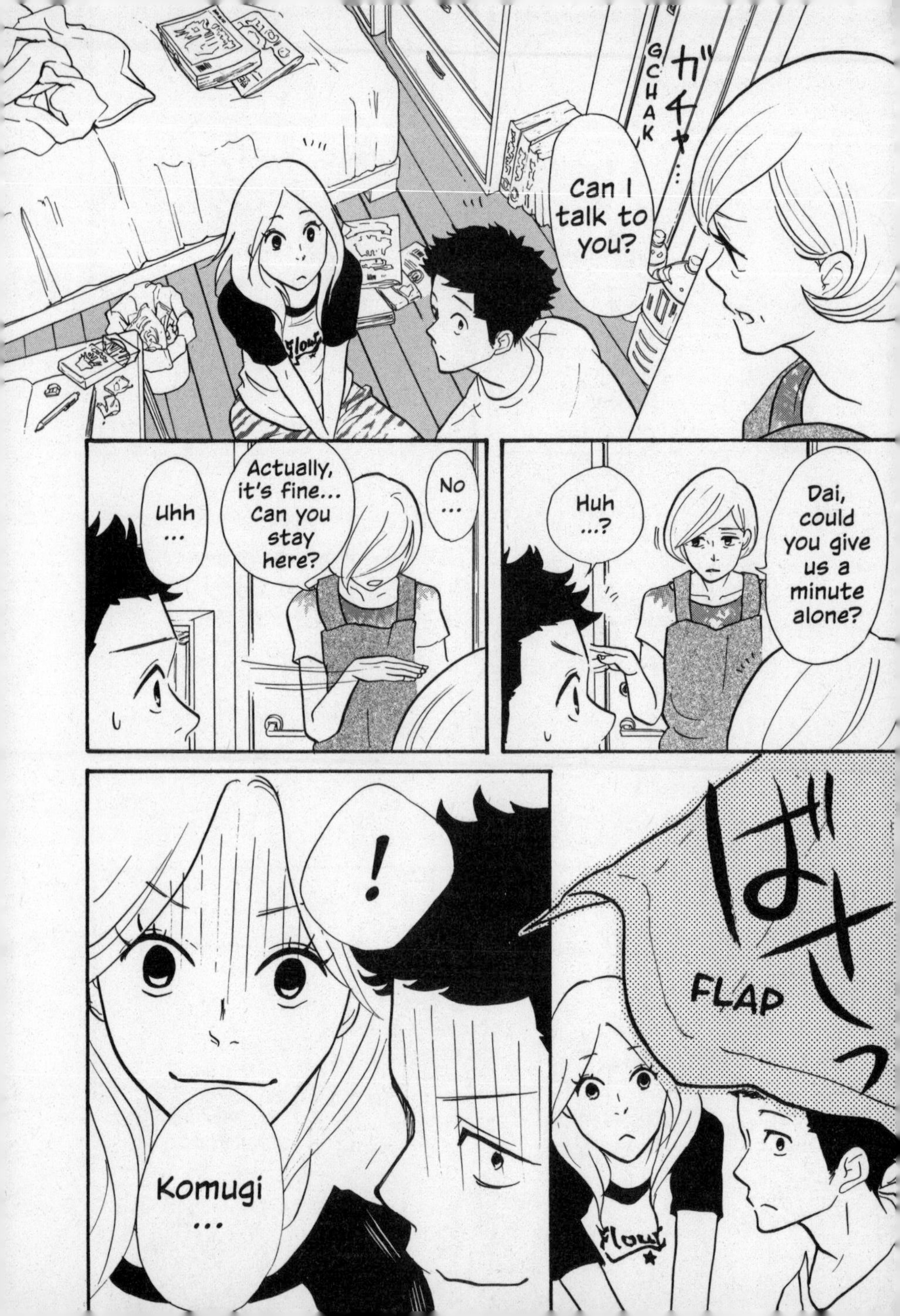
ガチャ…
GCHAK
Can I talk to you?
Dai, could you give us a minute alone?
Huh …?
No …
Actually, it's fine... Can you stay here?
Uhh …
ばさっ
FLAP
!
Komugi …

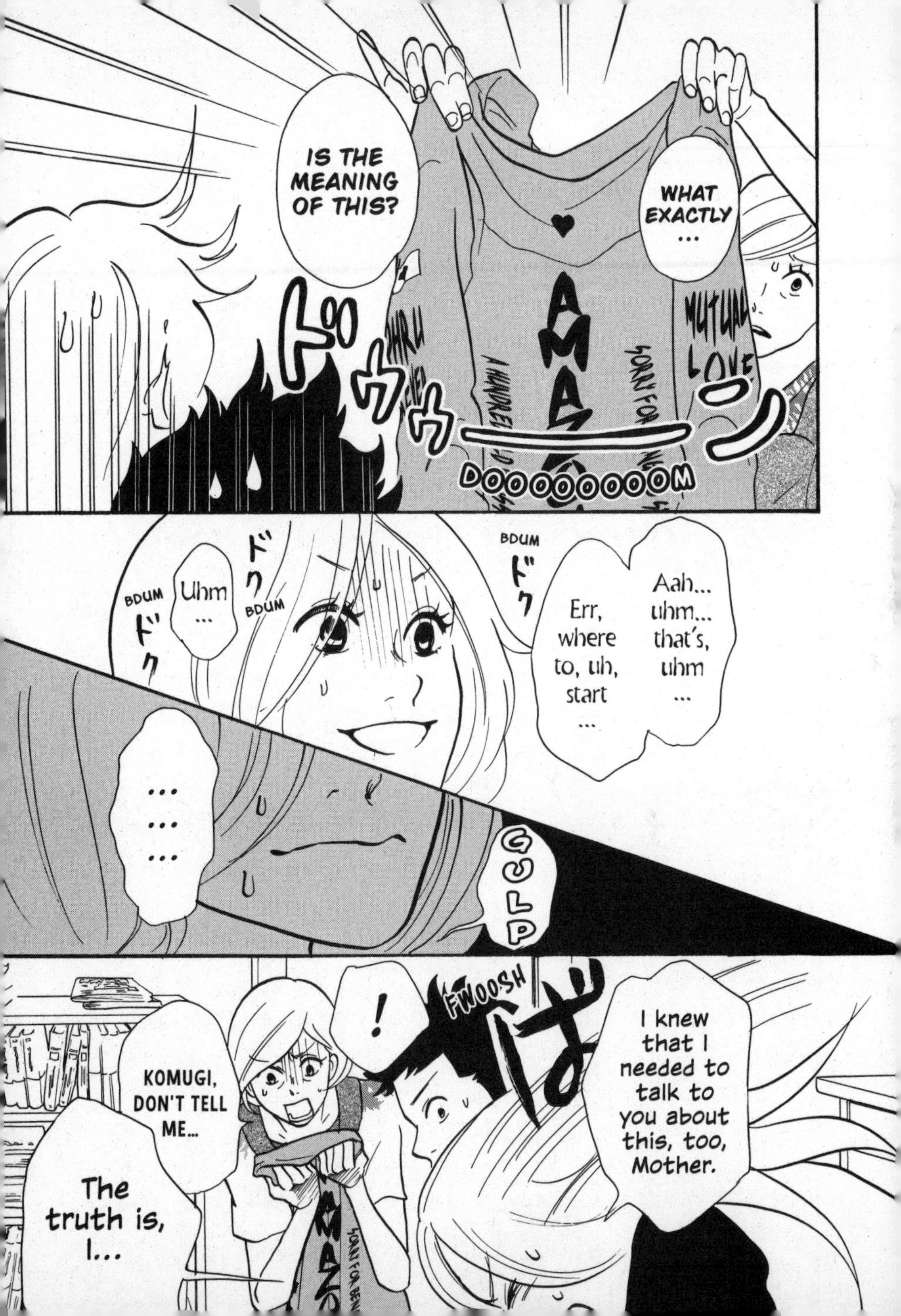

WHAT EXACTLY ...
IS THE MEANING OF THIS?
MUTUAL LOVE
DOOOOOOOOOM
BDUM
Aah... uhm... that's, uhm ...
Err, where to, uh, start ...
BDUM
Uhm ...
BDUM
... ...
GULP
I knew that I needed to talk to you about this, too, Mother.
FWOOSH
!
KOMUGI, DON'T TELL ME...
The truth is, I...

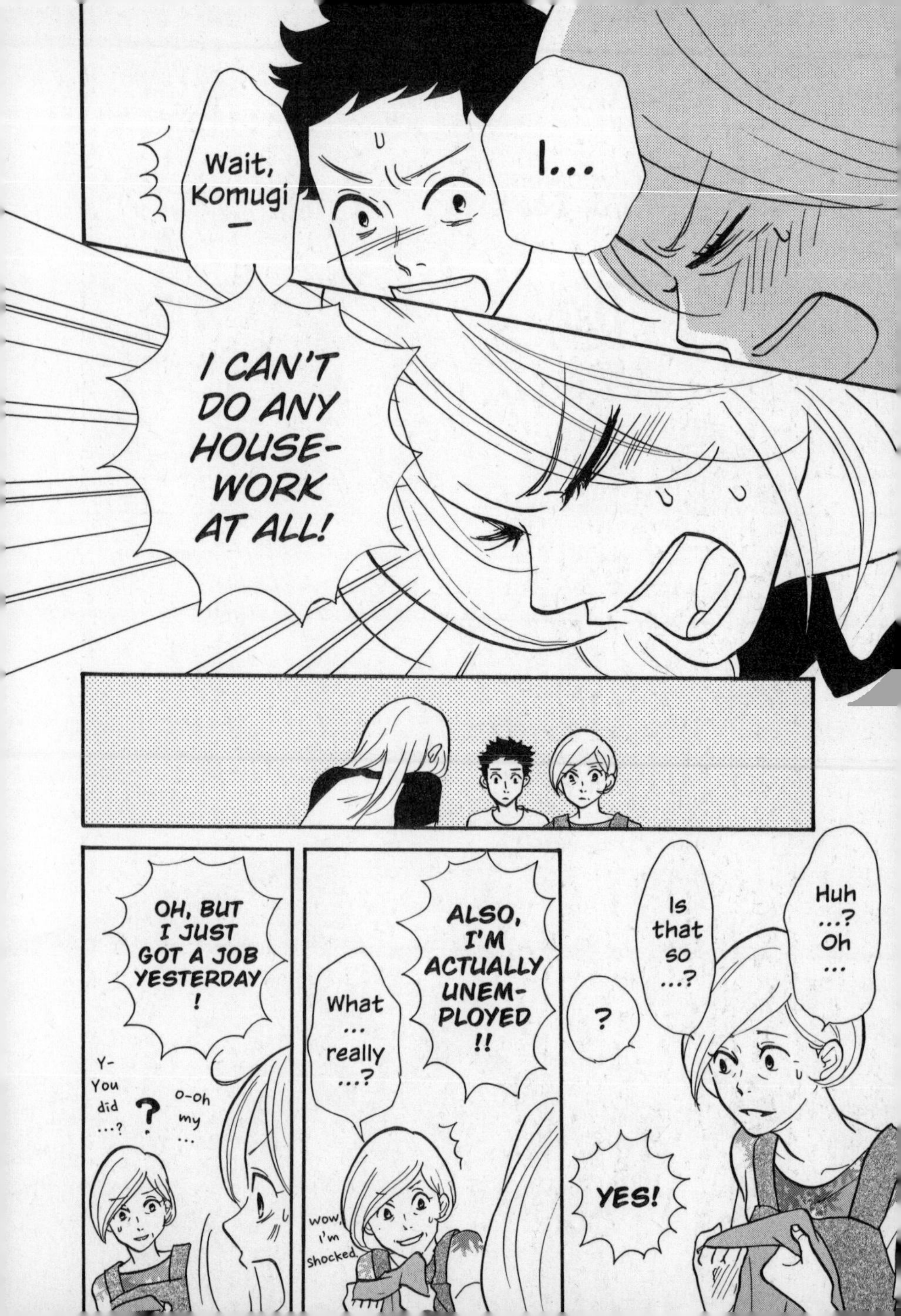
I...
Wait, Komugi —
I CAN'T DO ANY HOUSEWORK AT ALL!
Huh...? Oh...
Is that so...?
?
YES!
ALSO, I'M ACTUALLY UNEMPLOYED!!
What... really...?
wow, I'm shocked
OH, BUT I JUST GOT A JOB YESTERDAY!
O-oh my...
?
Y-You did...?

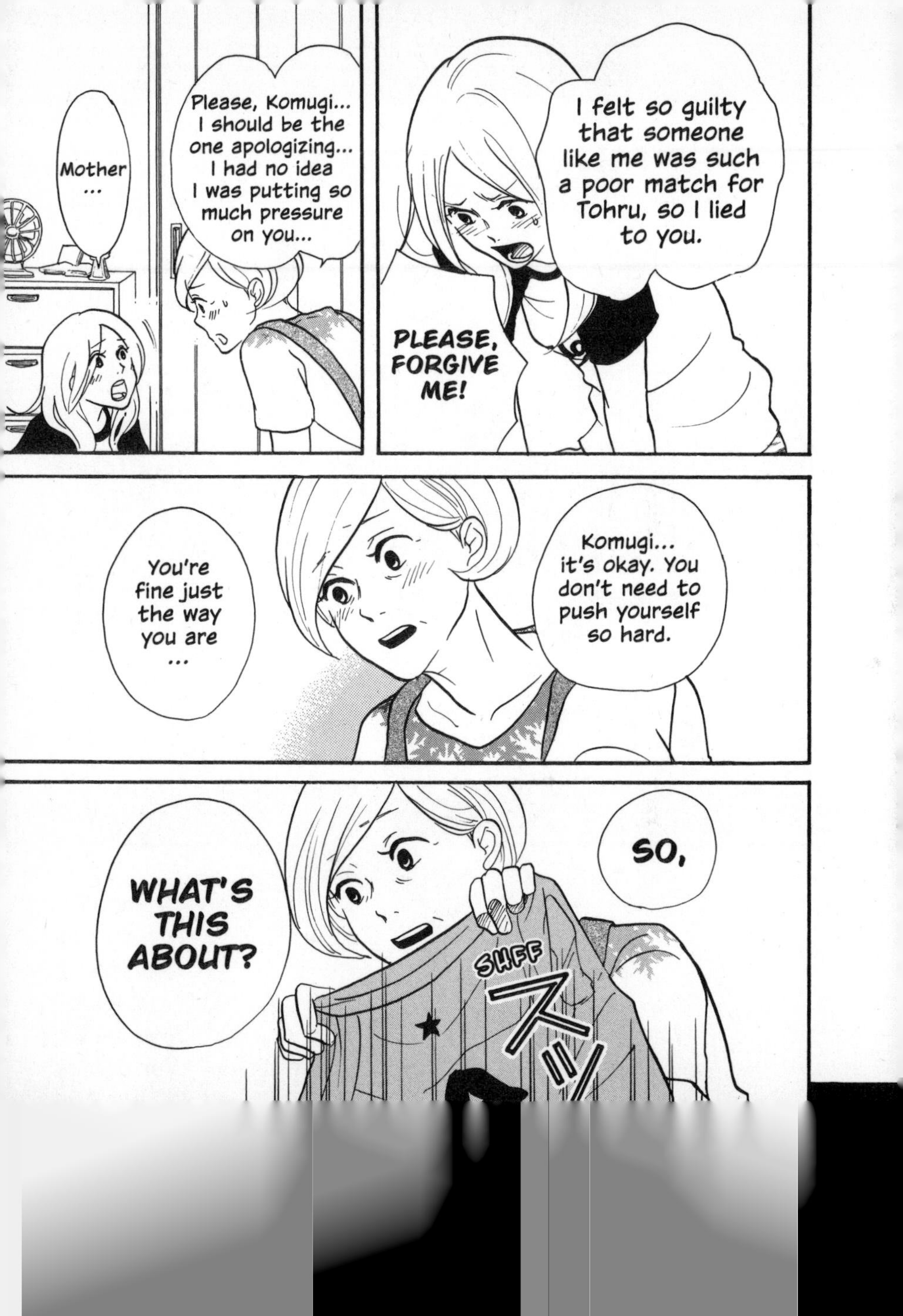
I felt so guilty that someone like me was such a poor match for Tohru, so I lied to you.
PLEASE, FORGIVE ME!
Please, Komugi... I should be the one apologizing... I had no idea I was putting so much pressure on you...
Mother ...
Komugi... it's okay. You don't need to push yourself so hard.
You're fine just the way you are ...
SO,
SHFF
WHAT'S THIS ABOUT?

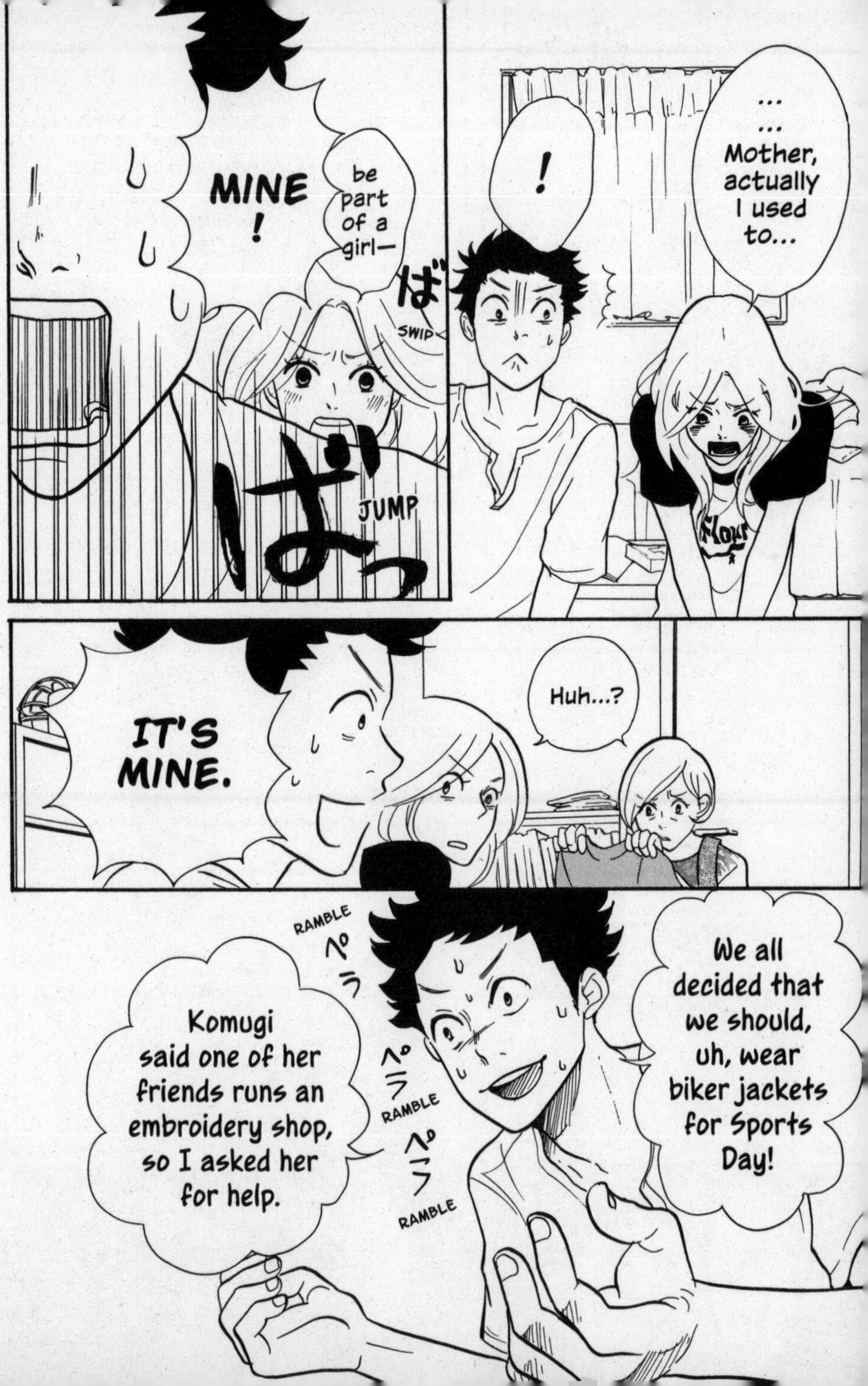
... ... Mother, actually I used to...
!
be part of a girl—
MINE!
ば
SWIP
ばっ
JUMP
Huh...?
IT'S MINE.
We all decided that we should, uh, wear biker jackets for Sports Day!
ペラ
RAMBLE
ペラ
RAMBLE
ペラ
RAMBLE
Komugi said one of her friends runs an embroidery shop, so I asked her for help.

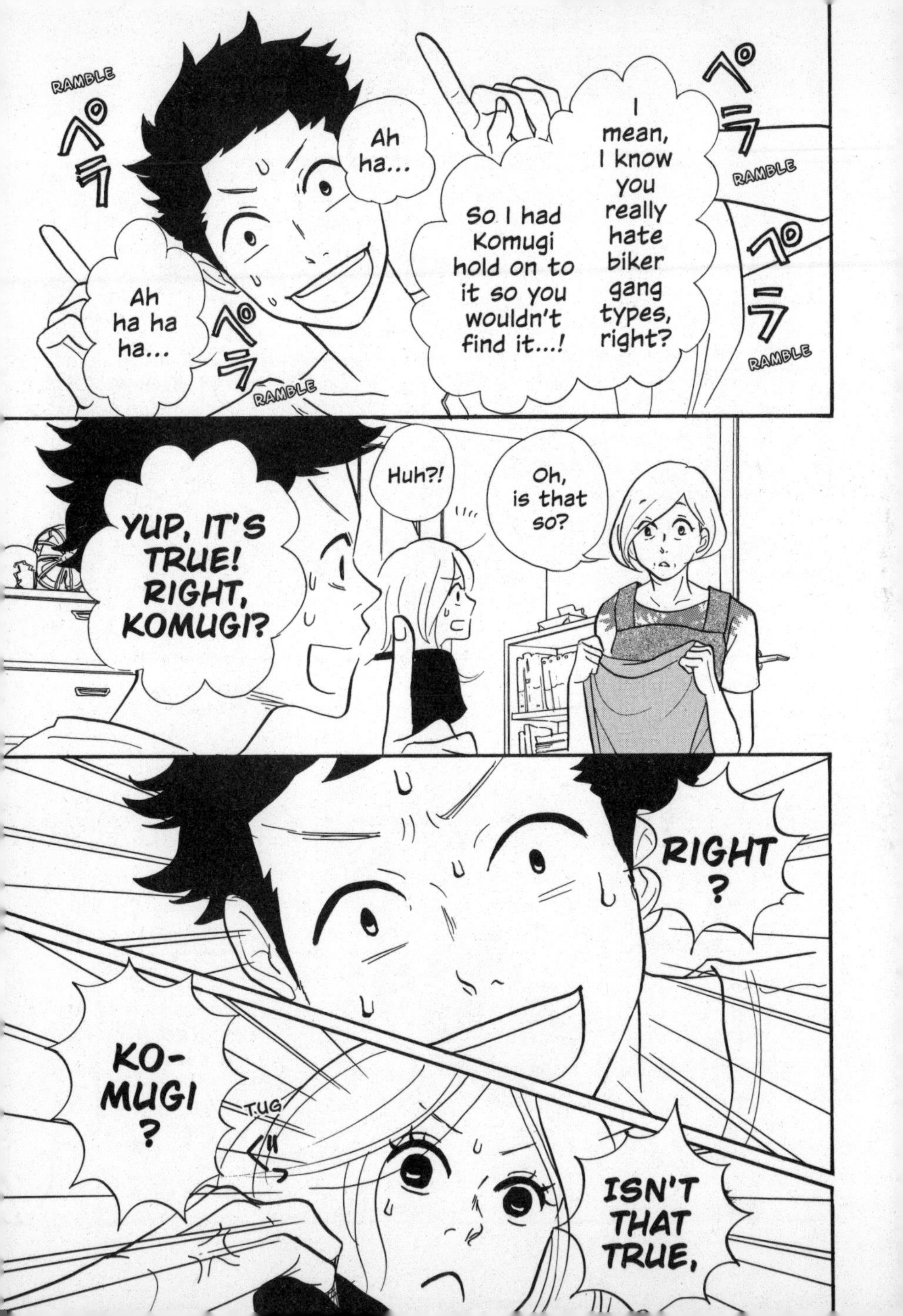
ペラ
RAMBLE
I mean, I know you really hate biker gang types, right?
So I had Komugi hold on to it so you wouldn't find it...!
Ah ha...
RAMBLE
ペラ
Ah ha ha ha...
ペラ
RAMBLE
ペラ
RAMBLE
ペラ
RAMBLE
Oh, is that so?
Huh?!
YUP, IT'S TRUE! RIGHT, KOMUGI?
RIGHT?
KO-MUGI?
TUG
ISN'T THAT TRUE,

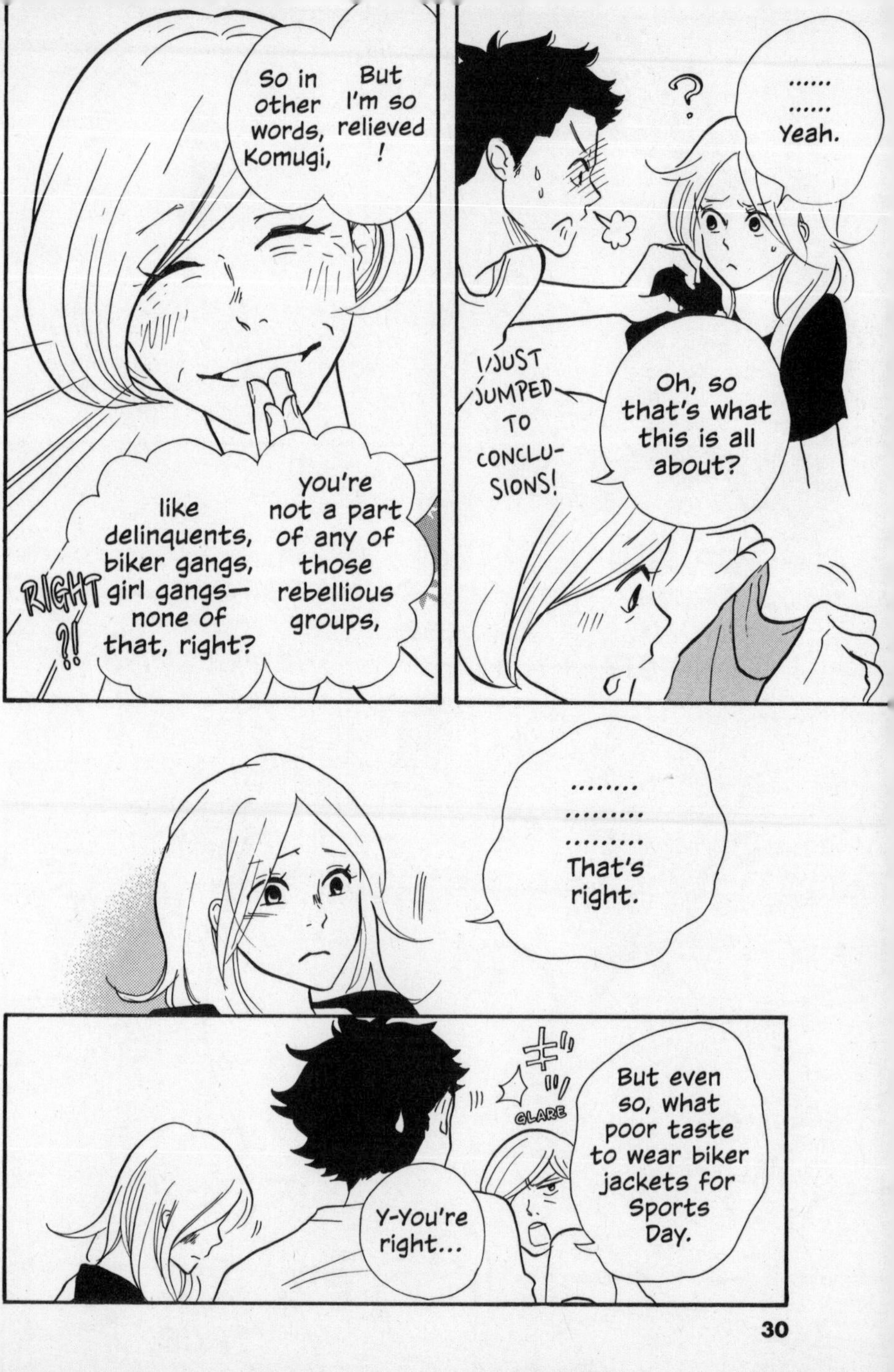
.... Yeah.
?
Oh, so that's what this is all about?
I/JUST JUMPED TO CONCLUSIONS!
But I'm so relieved!
So in other words, Komugi,
you're not a part of any of those rebellious groups,
like delinquents, biker gangs, girl gangs— none of that, right?
RIGHT ?!
.... That's right.
But even so, what poor taste to wear biker jackets for Sports Day.
GLARE
Y-You're right...

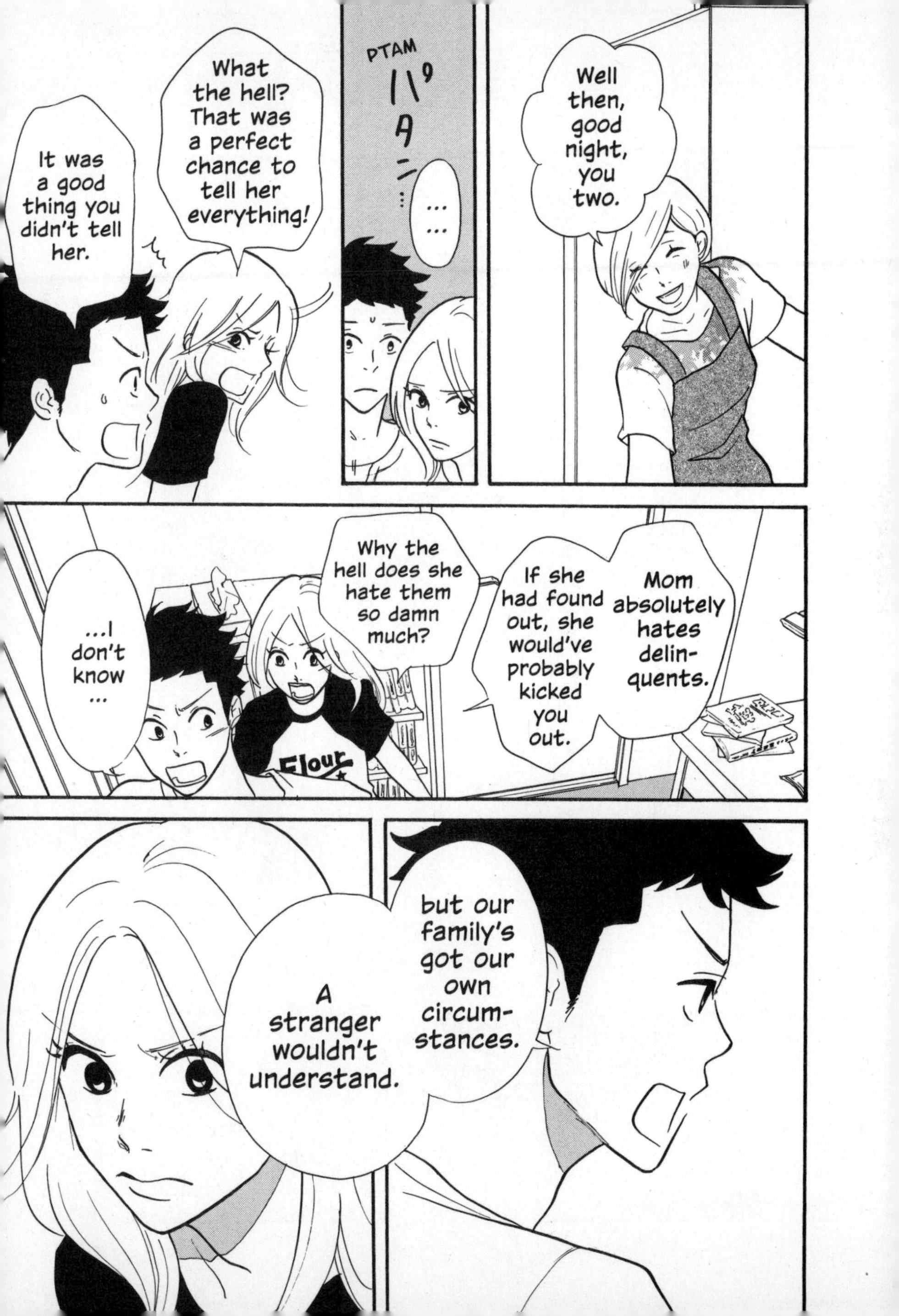
Well then, good night, you two.
PTAM
......
What the hell? That was a perfect chance to tell her everything!
It was a good thing you didn't tell her.
Mom absolutely hates delinquents.
If she had found out, she would've probably kicked you out.
Why the hell does she hate them so damn much?
...I don't know ...
Flour
A stranger wouldn't understand.
but our family's got our own circumstances.

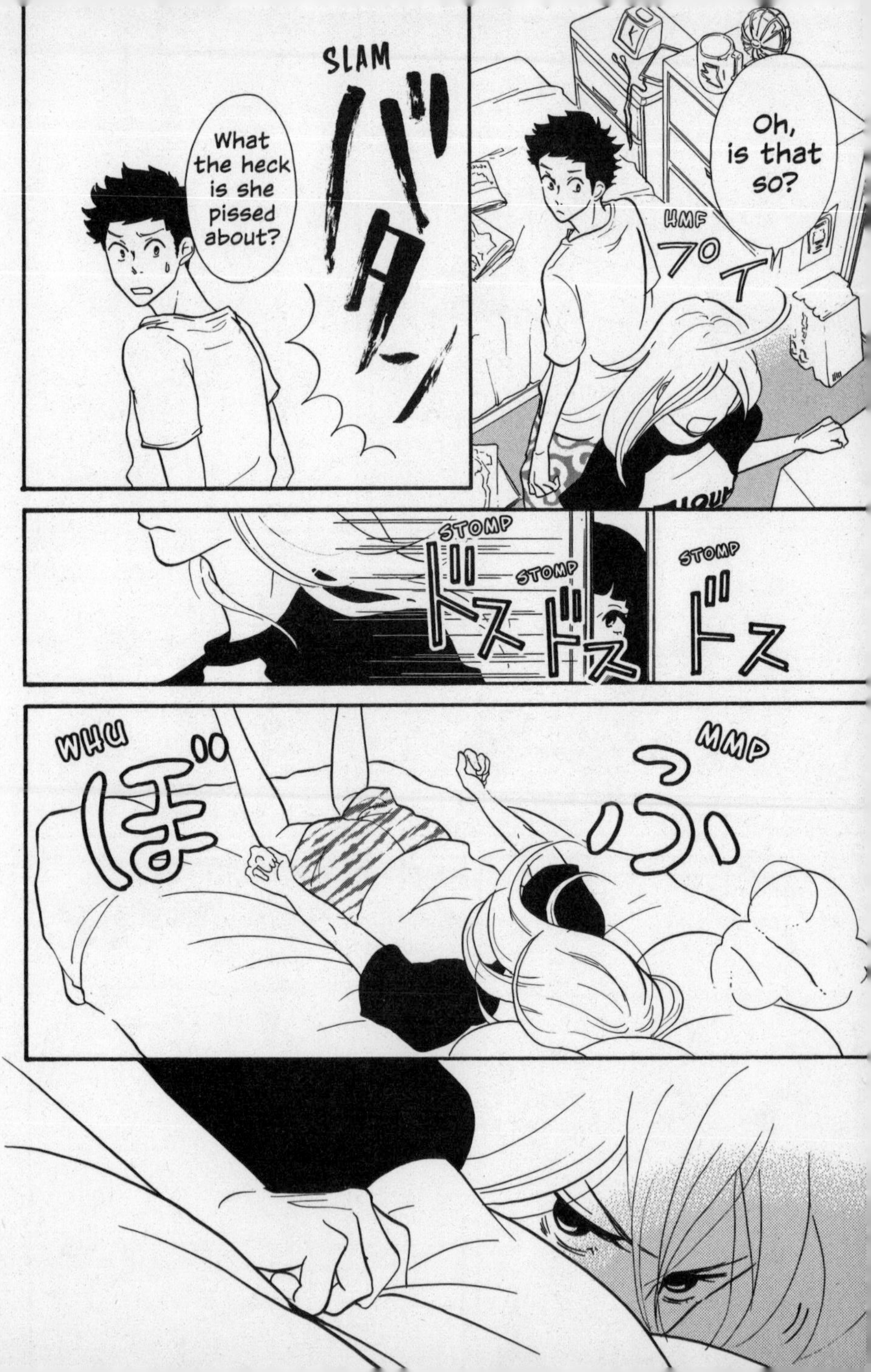
Oh, is that so?
HMF
プイ
SLAM
バタン
What the heck is she pissed about?
STOMP
ドス
STOMP
ドス
STOMP
ドス
WHU
ぼふっ
MMP

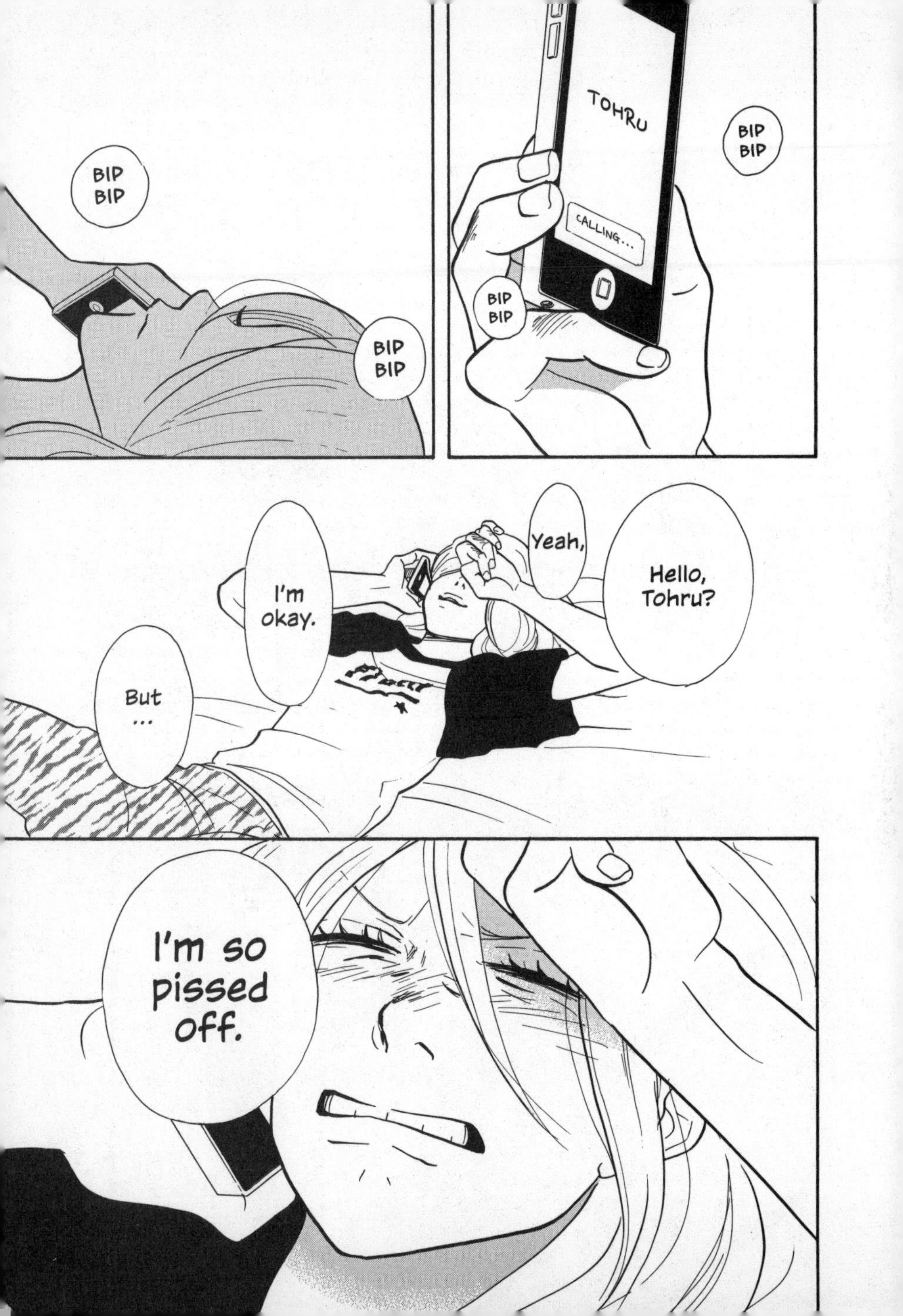
TOHRU
CALLING...
BIP BIP
BIP BIP
BIP BIP
BIP BIP
Hello, Tohru?
Yeah,
I'm okay.
But ...
I'm so pissed off.

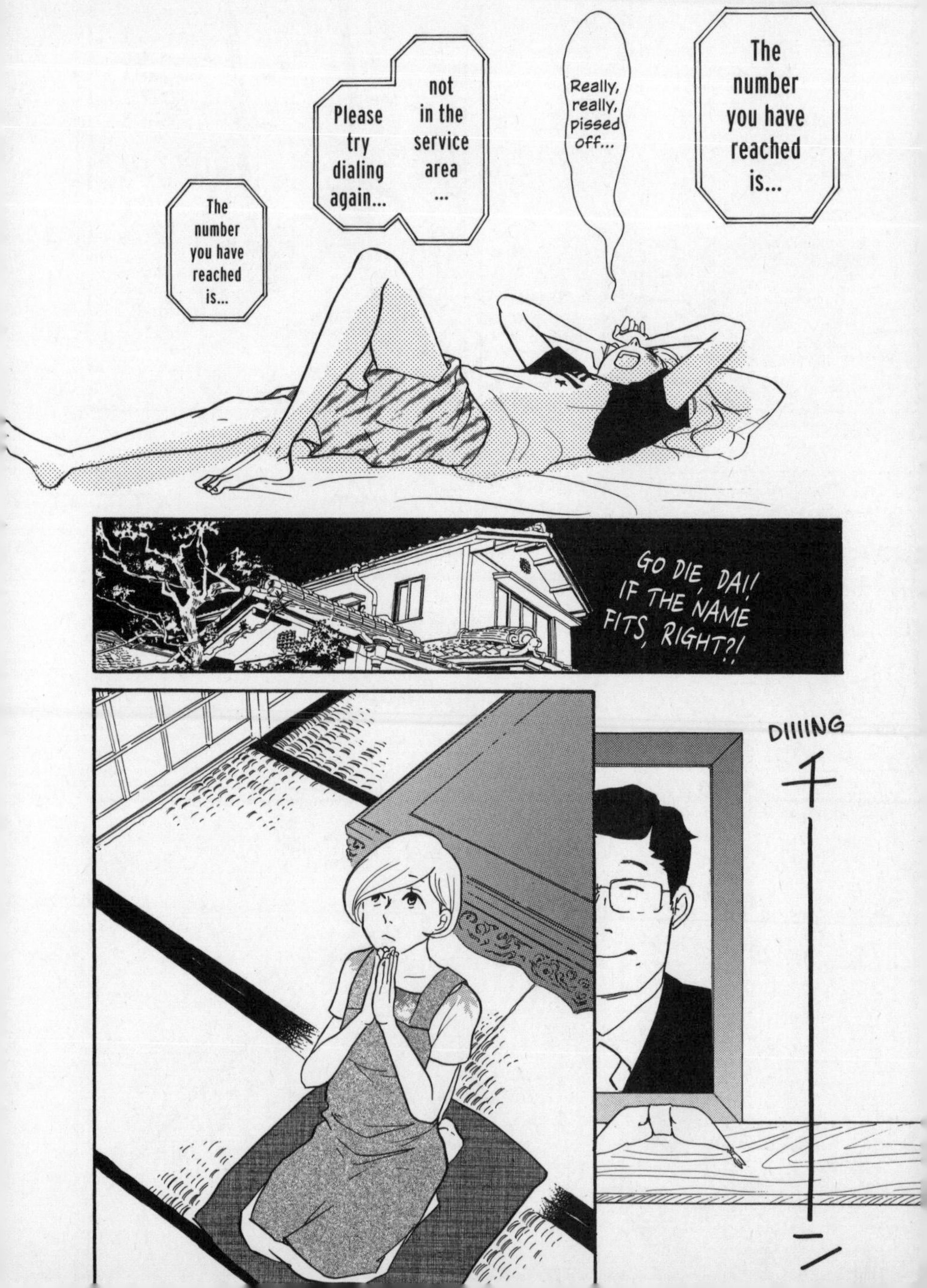
The number you have reached is...
Really, really, pissed off...
not in the service area ...
Please try dialing again...
The number you have reached is...
GO DIE, DAI! IF THE NAME FITS, RIGHT?!
DIIIING

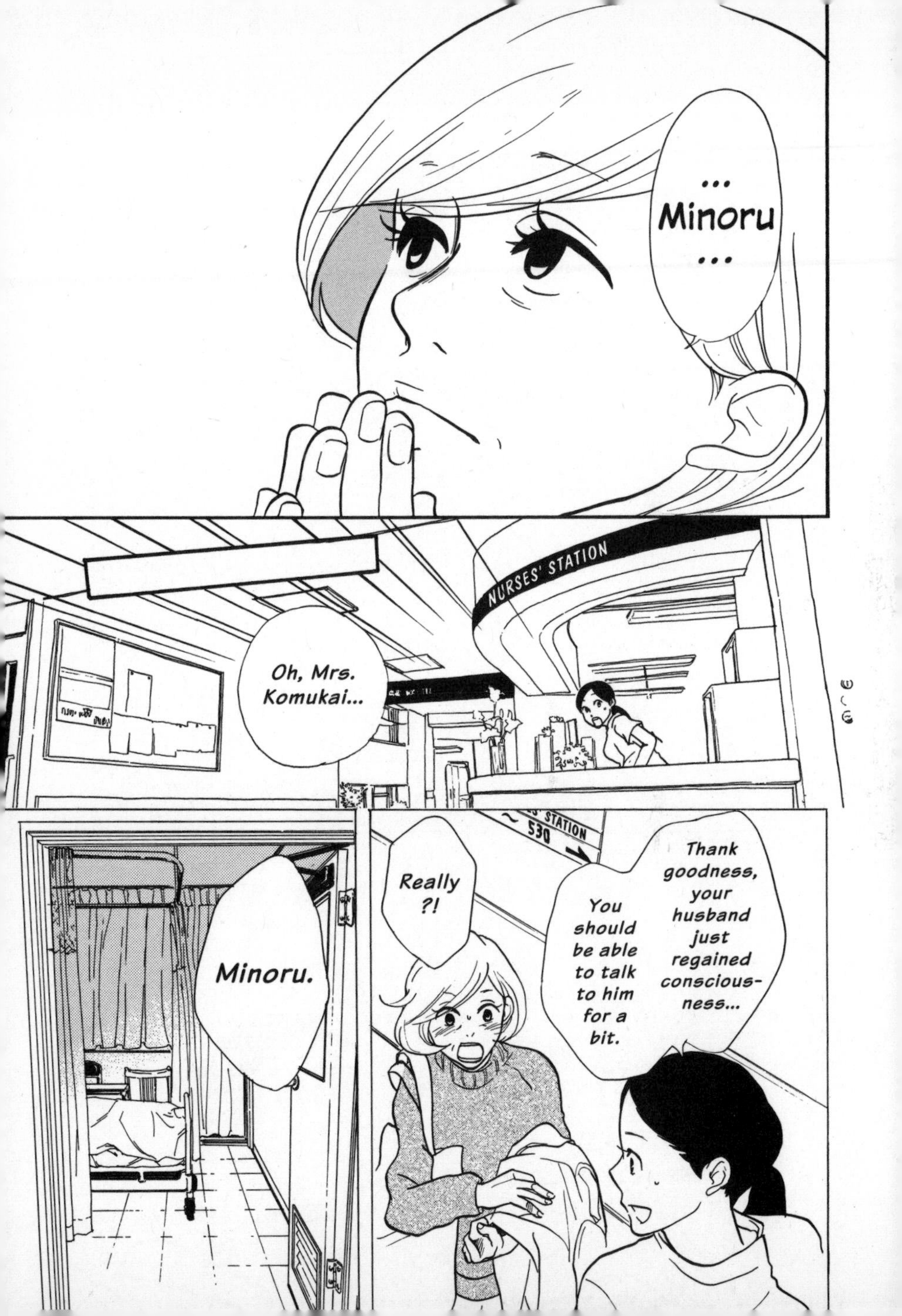

... Minoru ...
NURSES' STATION
Oh, Mrs. Komukai...
Thank goodness, your husband just regained conscious-ness...
You should be able to talk to him for a bit.
Really ?!
Minoru.

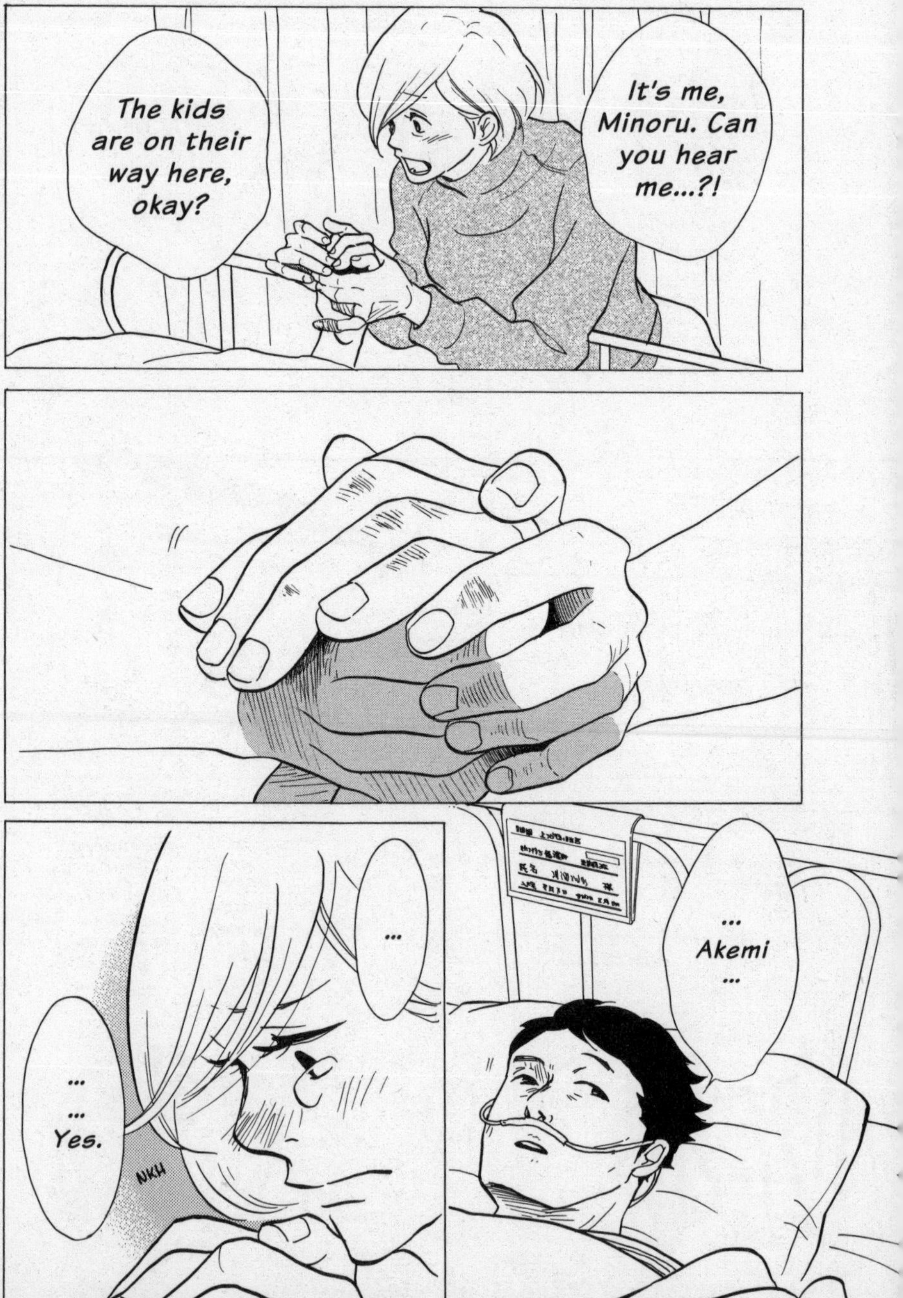
It's me, Minoru. Can you hear me...?!
The kids are on their way here, okay?
... Akemi ...
...
... ... Yes.
NKH

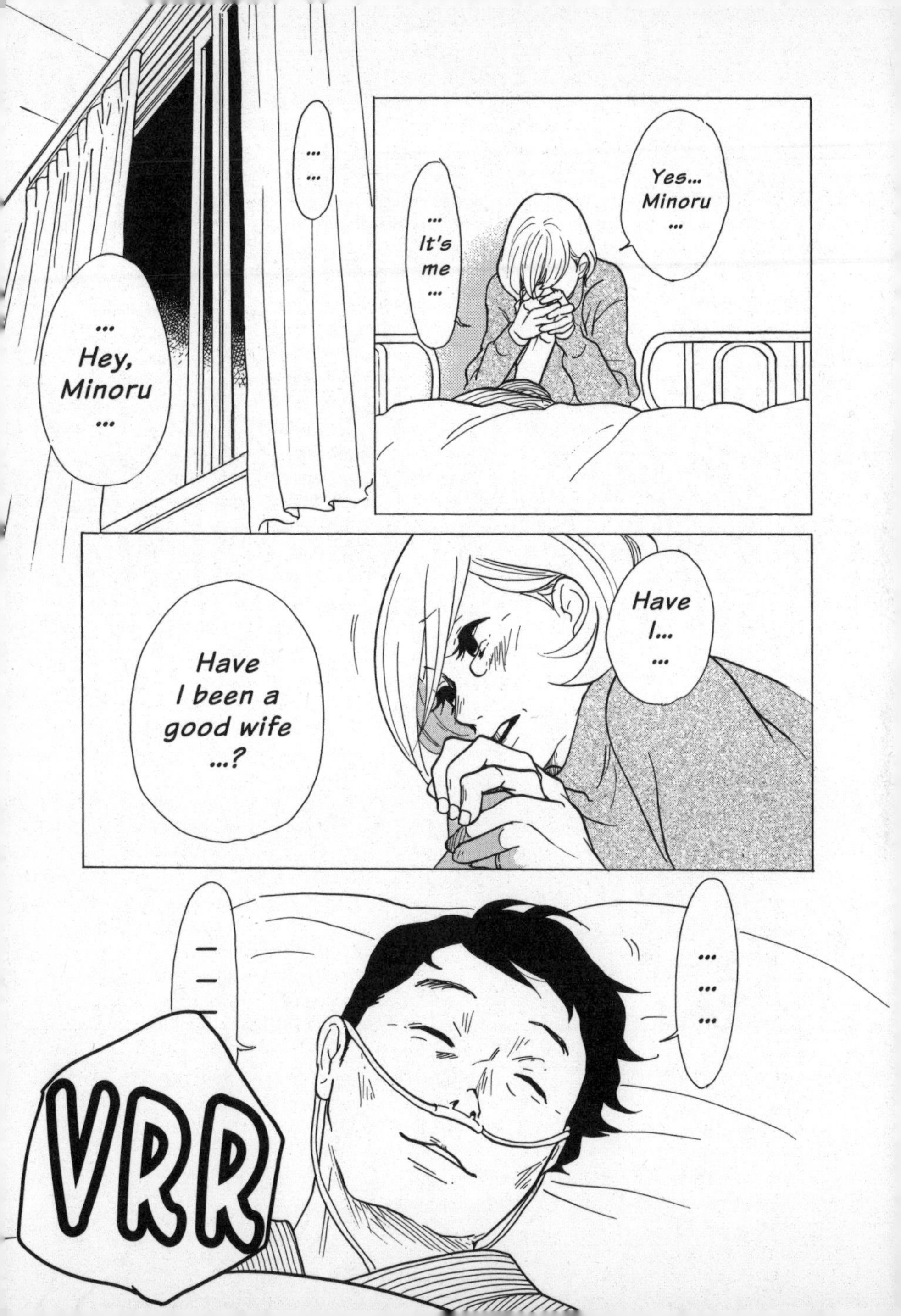
Yes... Minoru ...
... It's me ...
... ...
... Hey, Minoru ...
Have I... ...
Have I been a good wife ...?
... ...
— —
VRR

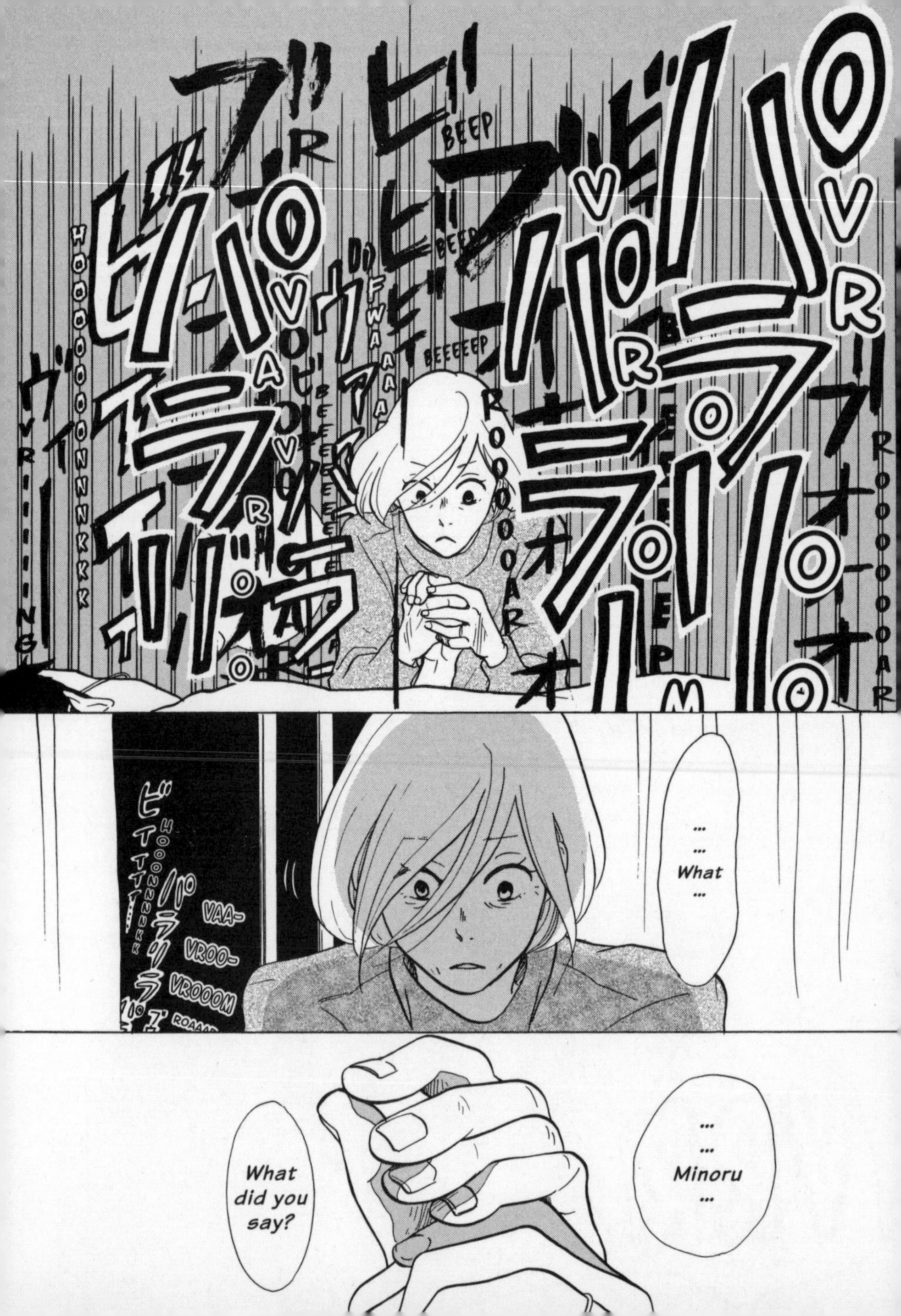
BEEP
BEEP
BEEEEEP
ROOOOOOAR
VAA-
VROO-
VROOOM
... ... What ...
... ... Minoru ...
What did you say?

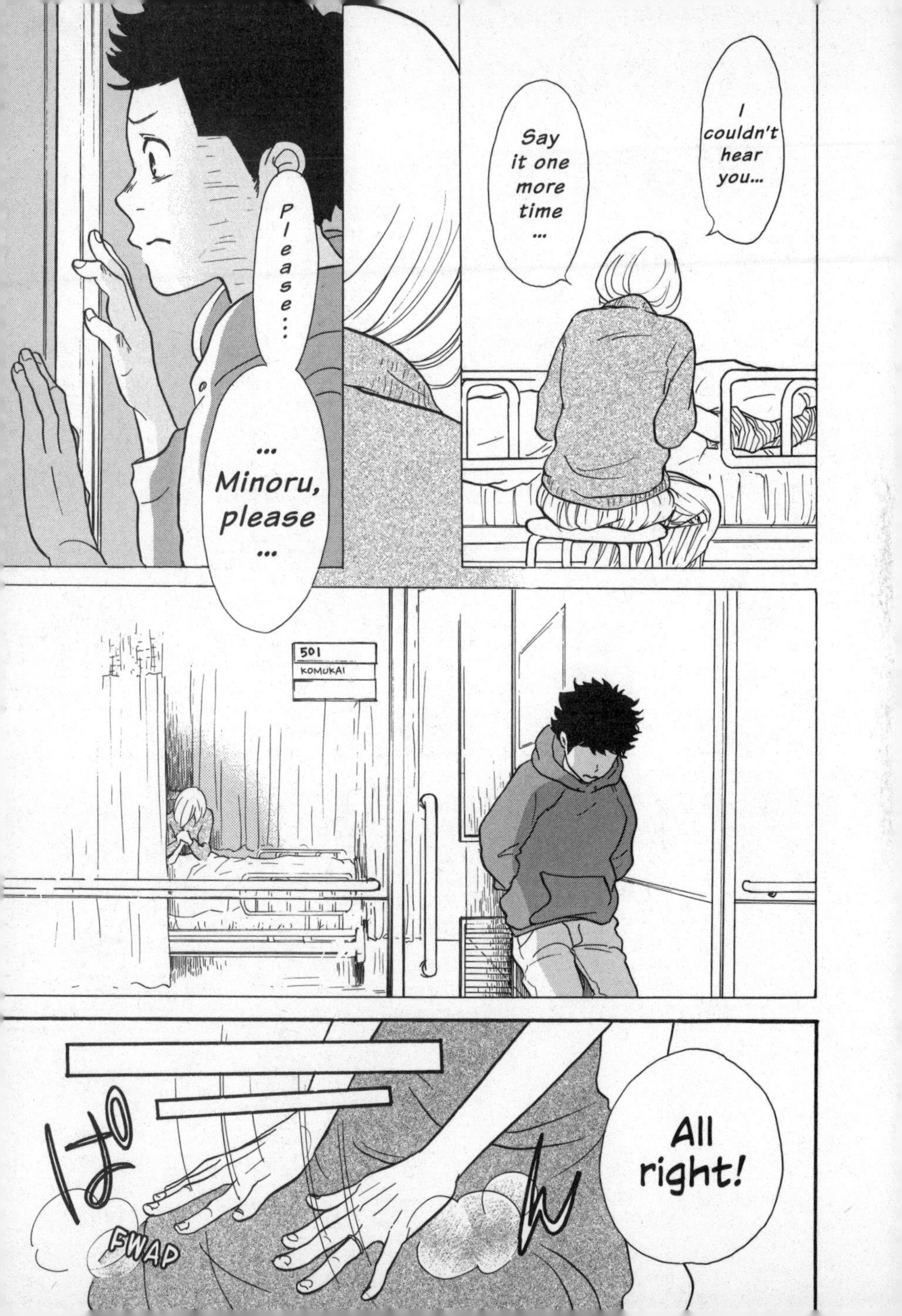
I couldn't hear you...
Say it one more time ...
Please...
... Minoru, please ...
501
KOMUKAI
All right!
FWAP

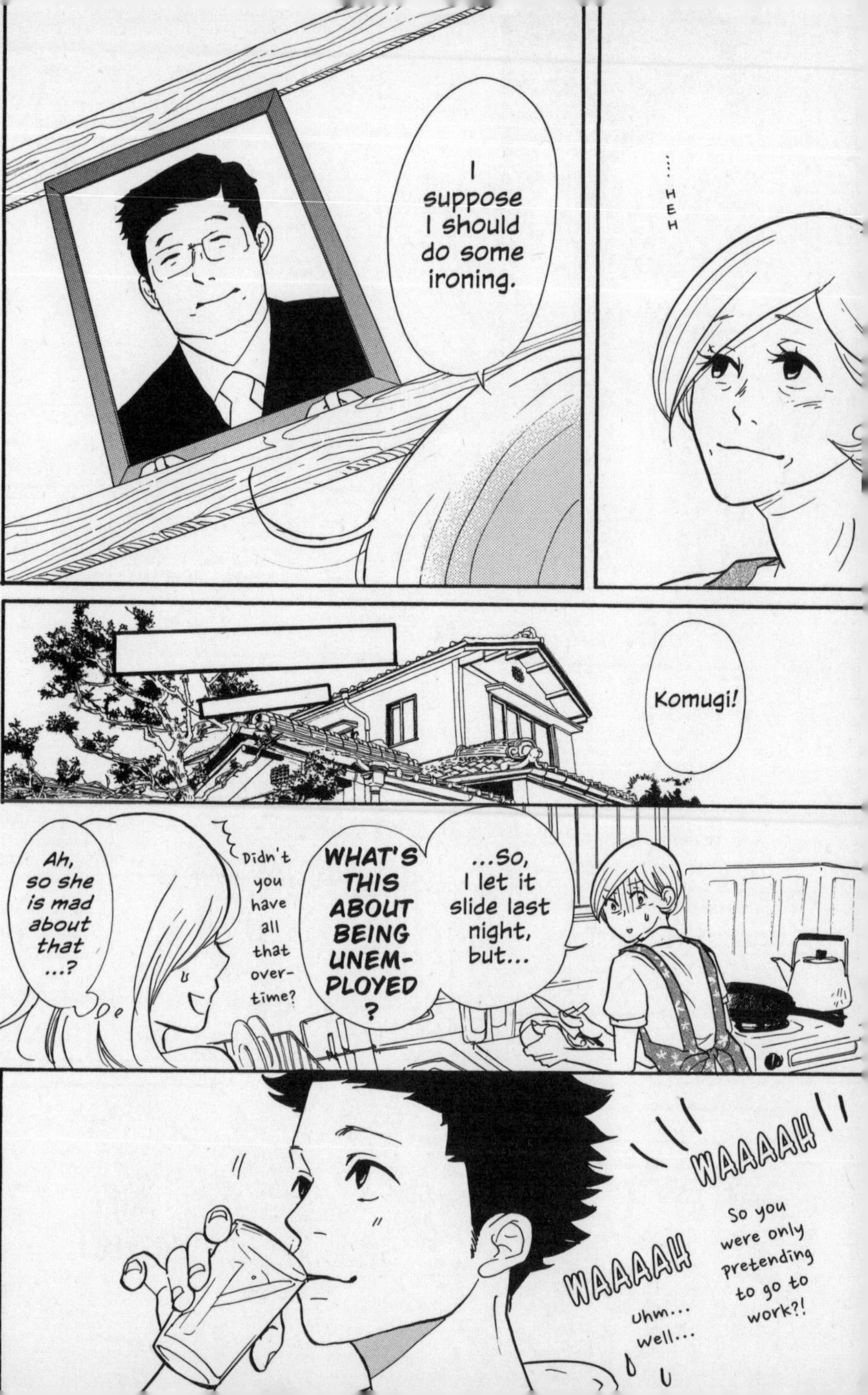
...HEH
I suppose I should do some ironing.
Komugi!
...So, I let it slide last night, but...
WHAT'S THIS ABOUT BEING UNEMPLOYED?
Didn't you have all that overtime?
Ah, so she is mad about that...?
WAAAAH
So you were only pretending to go to work?!
WAAAAH
Uhm... well...

11

SOMEONE I WANT TO DEFEAT

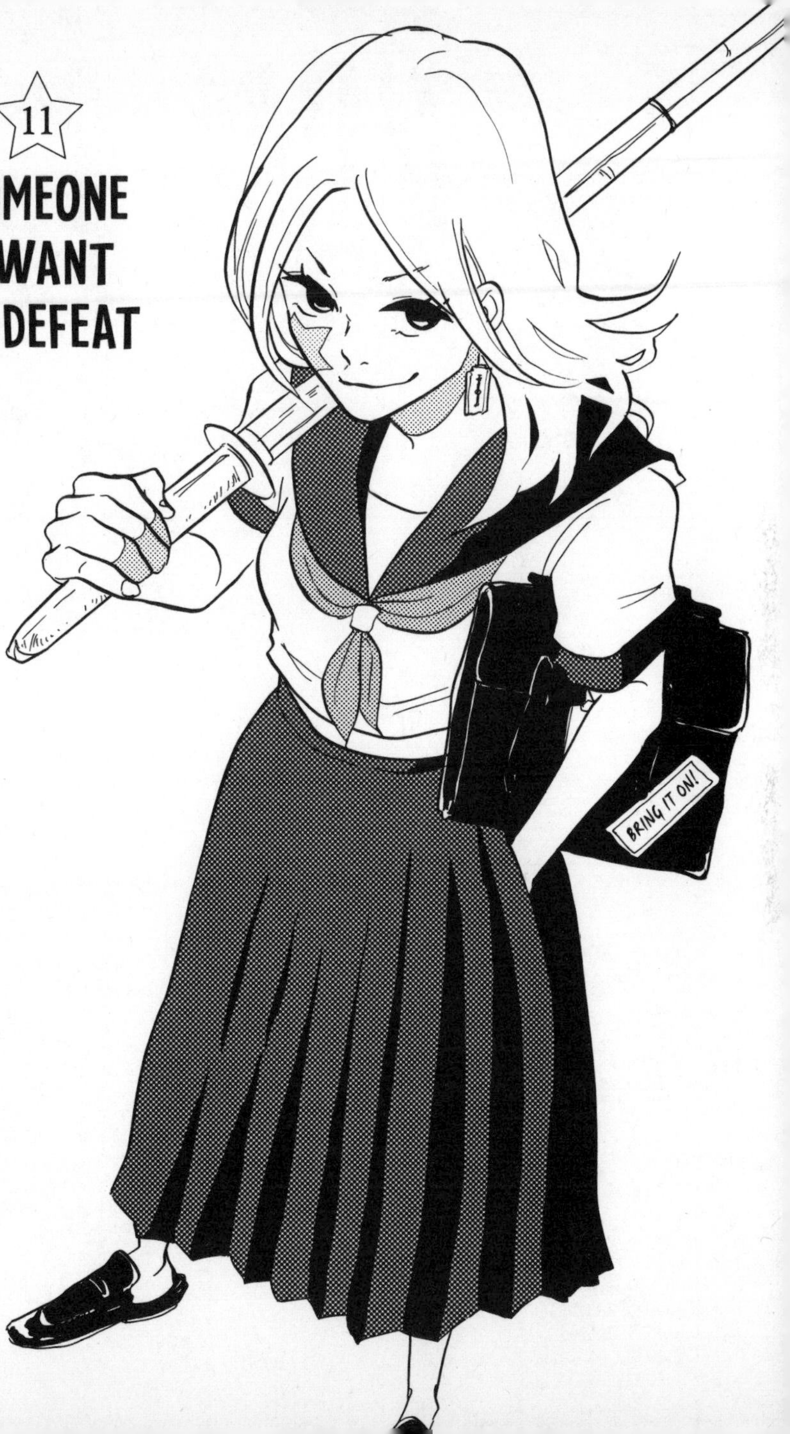
BRING IT ON!

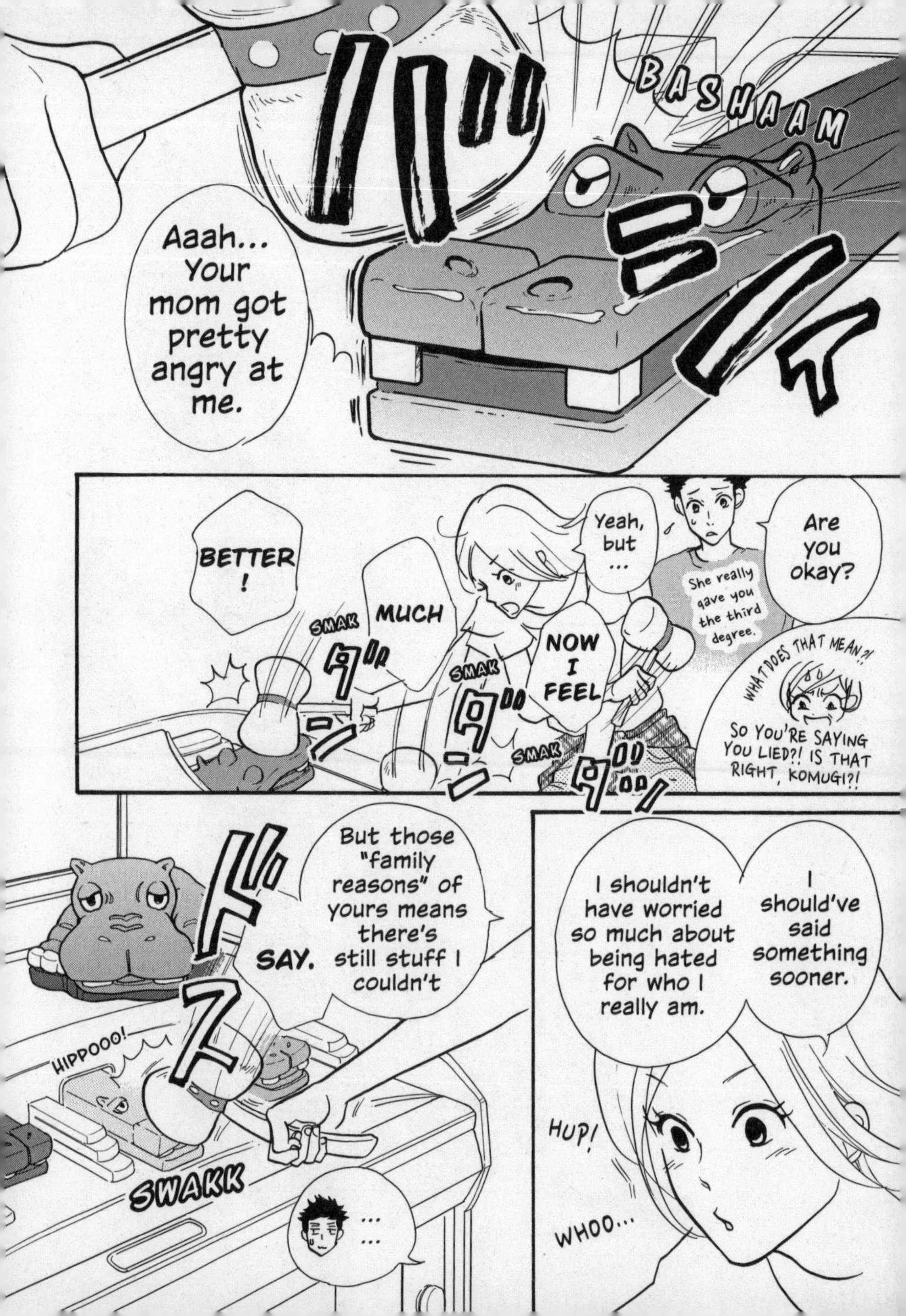
BASHAAM
Aaah... Your mom got pretty angry at me.
Are you okay?
She really gave you the third degree.
Yeah, but...
NOW I FEEL
MUCH
BETTER!
SMAK
SMAK
SMAK
WHAT DOES THAT MEAN?!
SO YOU'RE SAYING YOU LIED?! IS THAT RIGHT, KOMUGI?!
I should've said something sooner.
I shouldn't have worried so much about being hated for who I really am.
HUP!
WHOO...
But those "family reasons" of yours means there's still stuff I couldn't
SAY.
HIPPOOO!
SWAKK
... ...

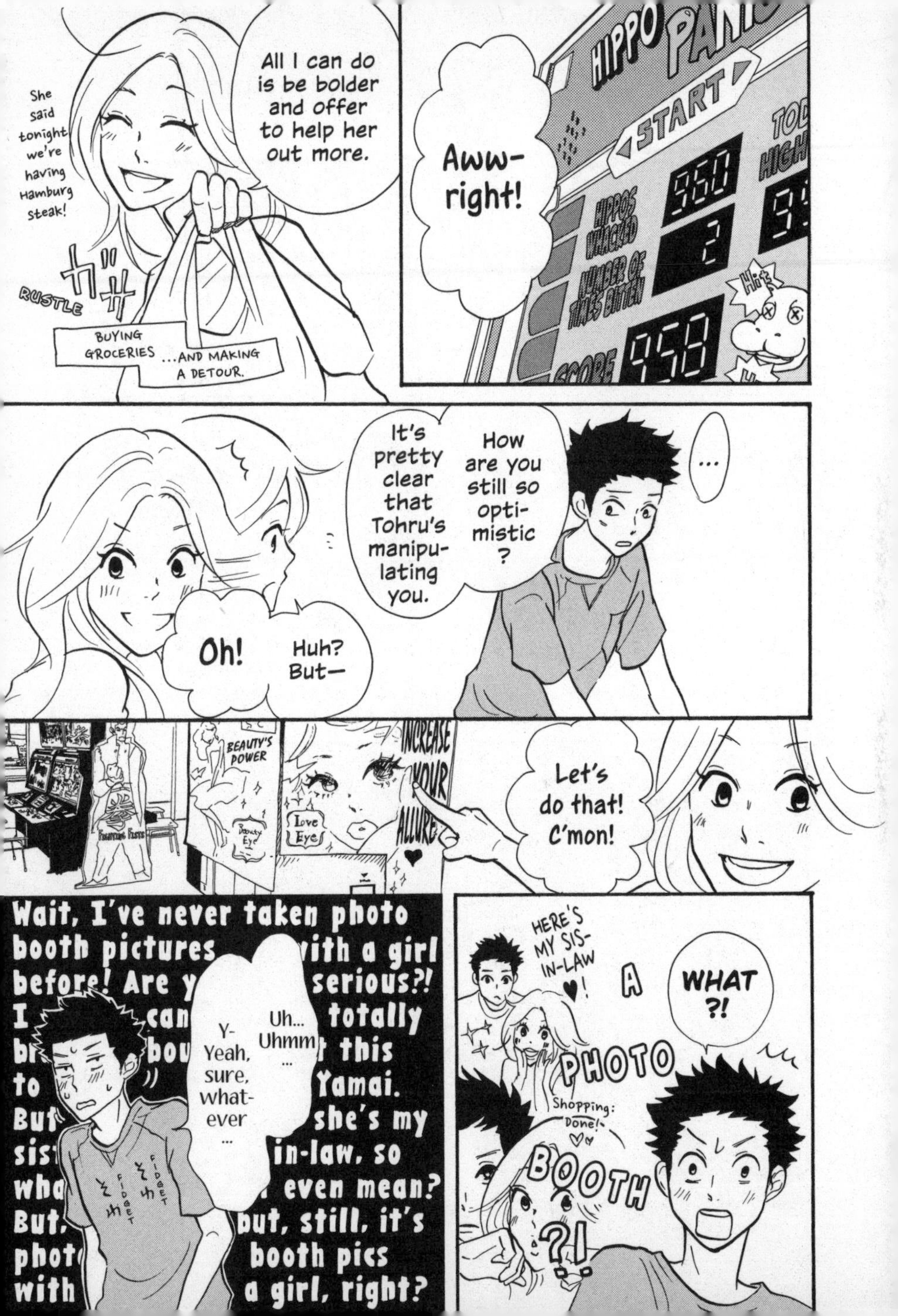
HIPPO PANIC
START
Aww-right!
HIPPOS WHACKED
NUMBER OF TIMES BITTEN
SCORE
960
2
958
Hit
All I can do is be bolder and offer to help her out more.
She said tonight we're having Hamburg steak!
RUSTLE
BUYING GROCERIES ...AND MAKING A DETOUR.
...
How are you still so opti-mistic?
It's pretty clear that Tohru's manipu-lating you.
Huh? But—
Oh!
Let's do that! C'mon!
INCREASE YOUR ALLURE
BEAUTY'S POWER
Love Eye
Beauty Eye
WHAT?!
A
HERE'S MY SIS-IN-LAW ♥!
PHOTO
Shopping: Done! ♥
BOOTH
?!
Wait, I've never taken photo
booth pictures with a girl
before! Are y serious?!
I can totally
br bou this
to Yamai.
But she's my
sis in-law, so
wha even mean?
But, but, still, it's
phot booth pics
with a girl, right?
Uh... Uhmm...
Y-Yeah, sure, whatever...
FIDGET FIDGET

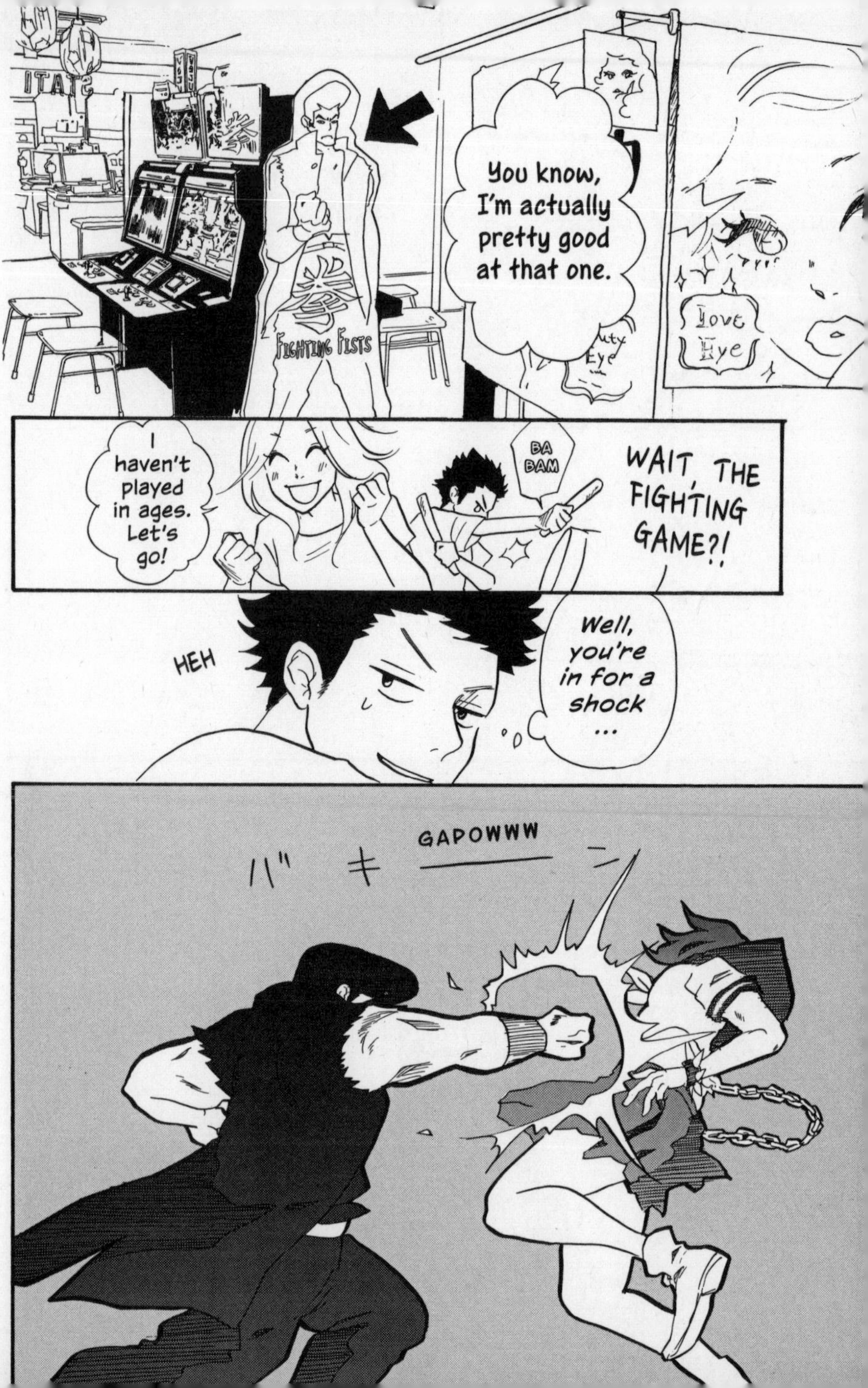
You know, I'm actually pretty good at that one.
Love Eye
FIGHTING FISTS
WAIT, THE FIGHTING GAME?!
BA BAM
I haven't played in ages. Let's go!
Well, you're in for a shock ...
HEH
GAPOWWW
バキーン

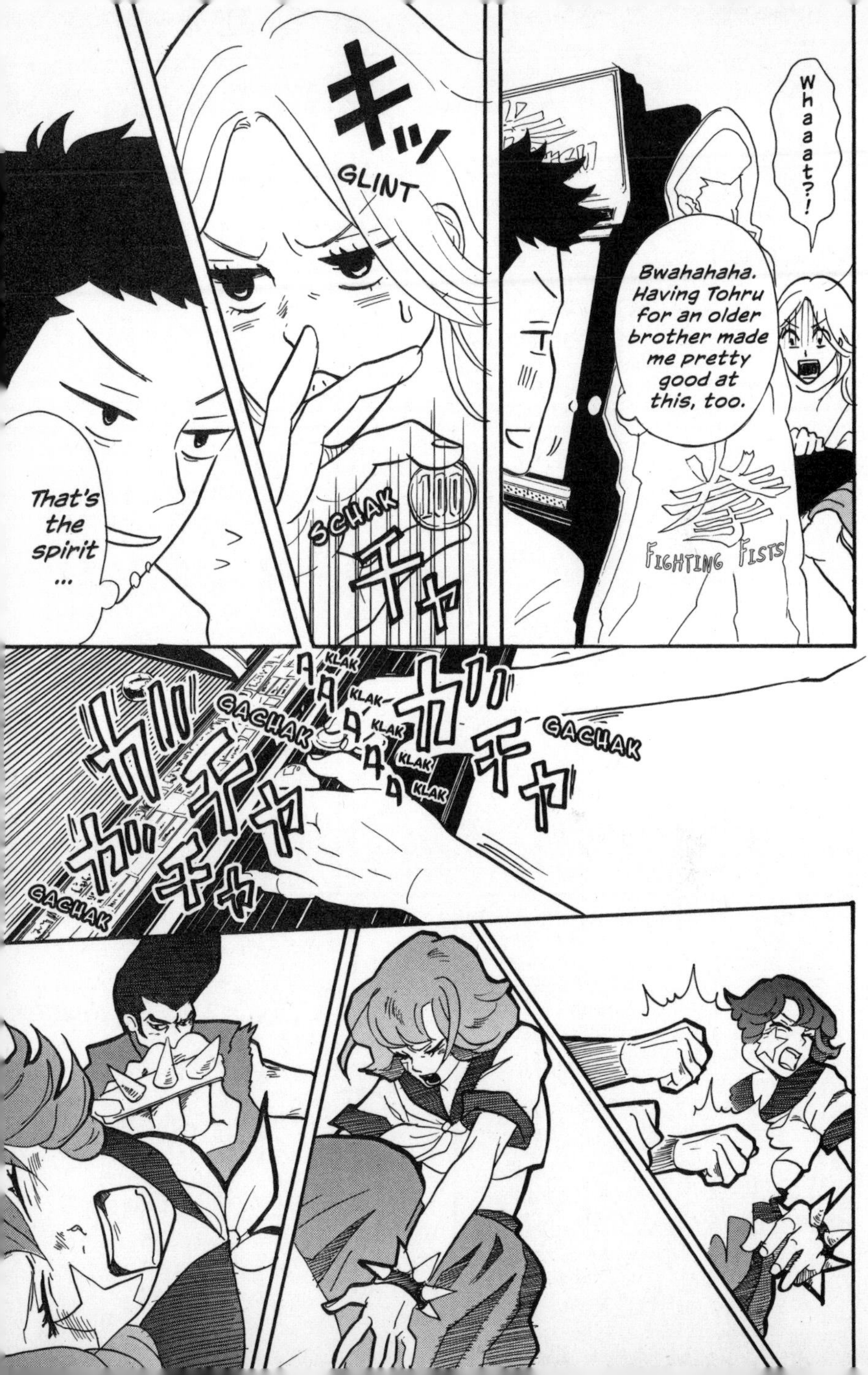

Whaaaat?!
Bwahahaha. Having Tohru for an older brother made me pretty good at this, too.
FIGHTING FISTS
キッ
GLINT
SCHAK
チャ
That's the spirit ...
GACHAK
KLAK
KLAK
KLAK
KLAK
KLAK
GACHAK
GACHAK

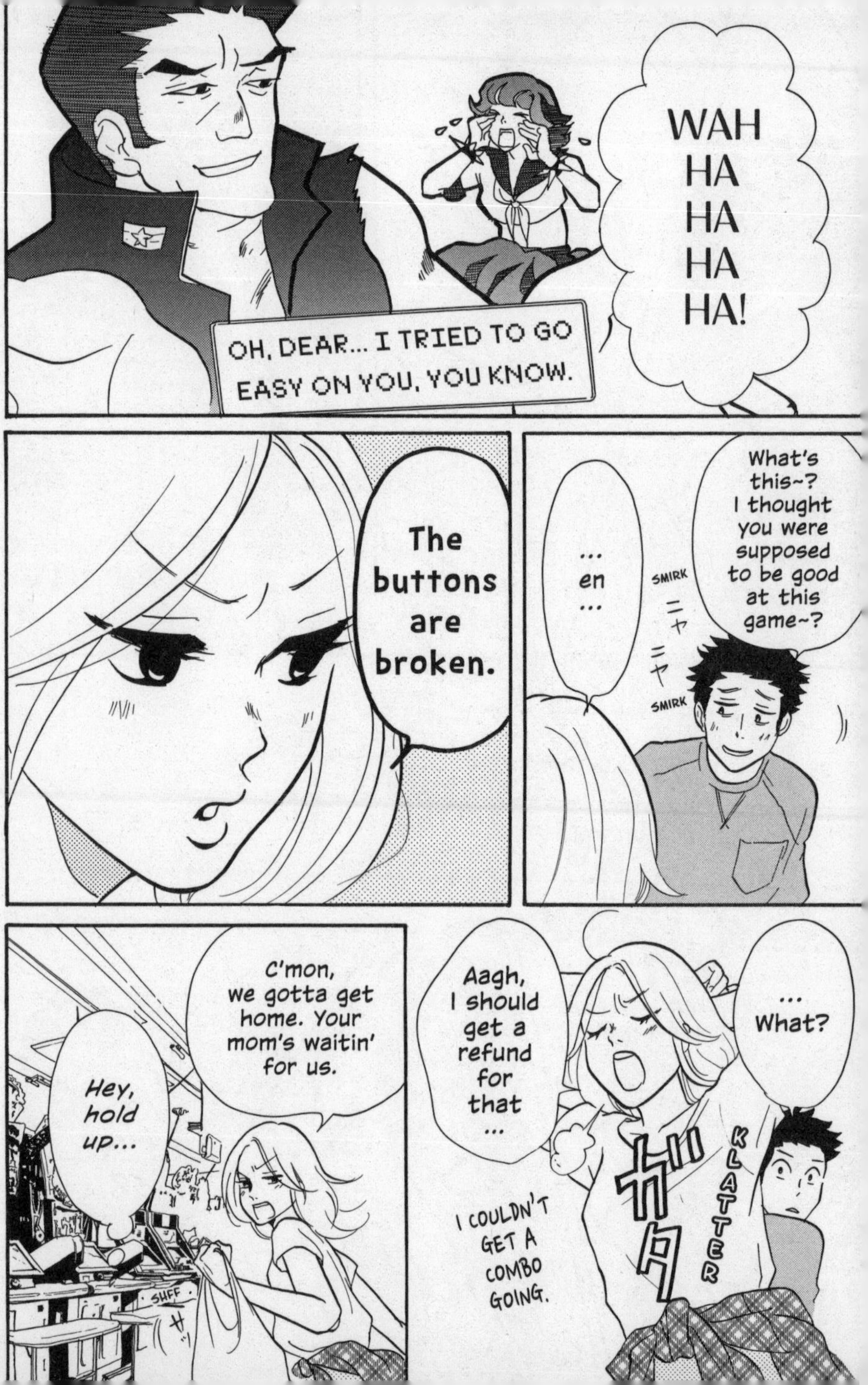
WAH HA HA HA HA!
OH, DEAR... I TRIED TO GO EASY ON YOU, YOU KNOW.
What's this~? I thought you were supposed to be good at this game~?
SMIRK
ニヤ
ニヤ
SMIRK
... en ...
The buttons are broken.
... What?
KLATTER
Aagh, I should get a refund for that ...
I COULDN'T GET A COMBO GOING.
C'mon, we gotta get home. Your mom's waitin' for us.
Hey, hold up...
SHFF

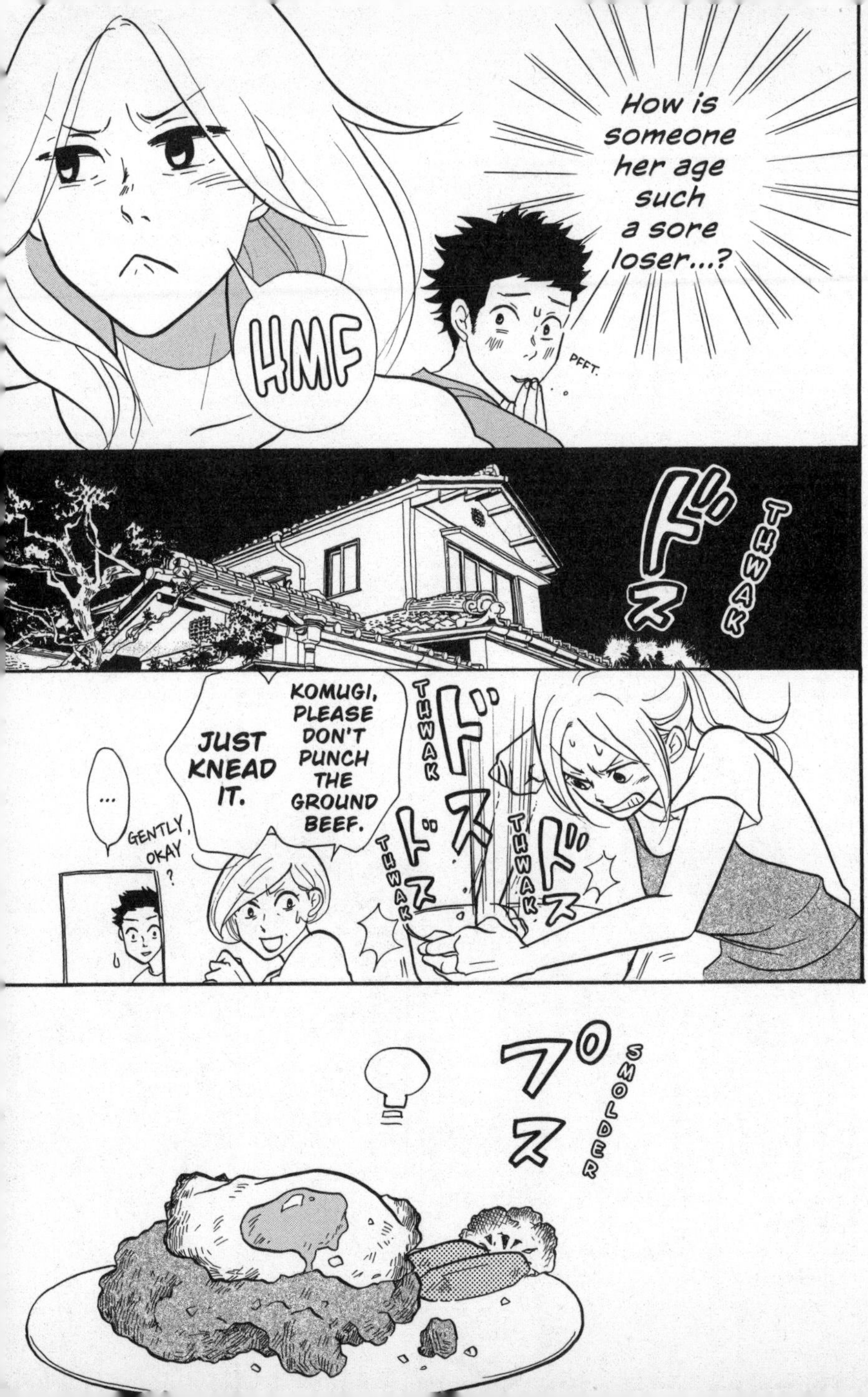
How is someone her age such a sore loser...?
PFFT.
HMF
THWAK
THWAK
THWAK
THWAK
KOMUGI, PLEASE DON'T PUNCH THE GROUND BEEF.
JUST KNEAD IT.
GENTLY, OKAY?
...
SMOLDER

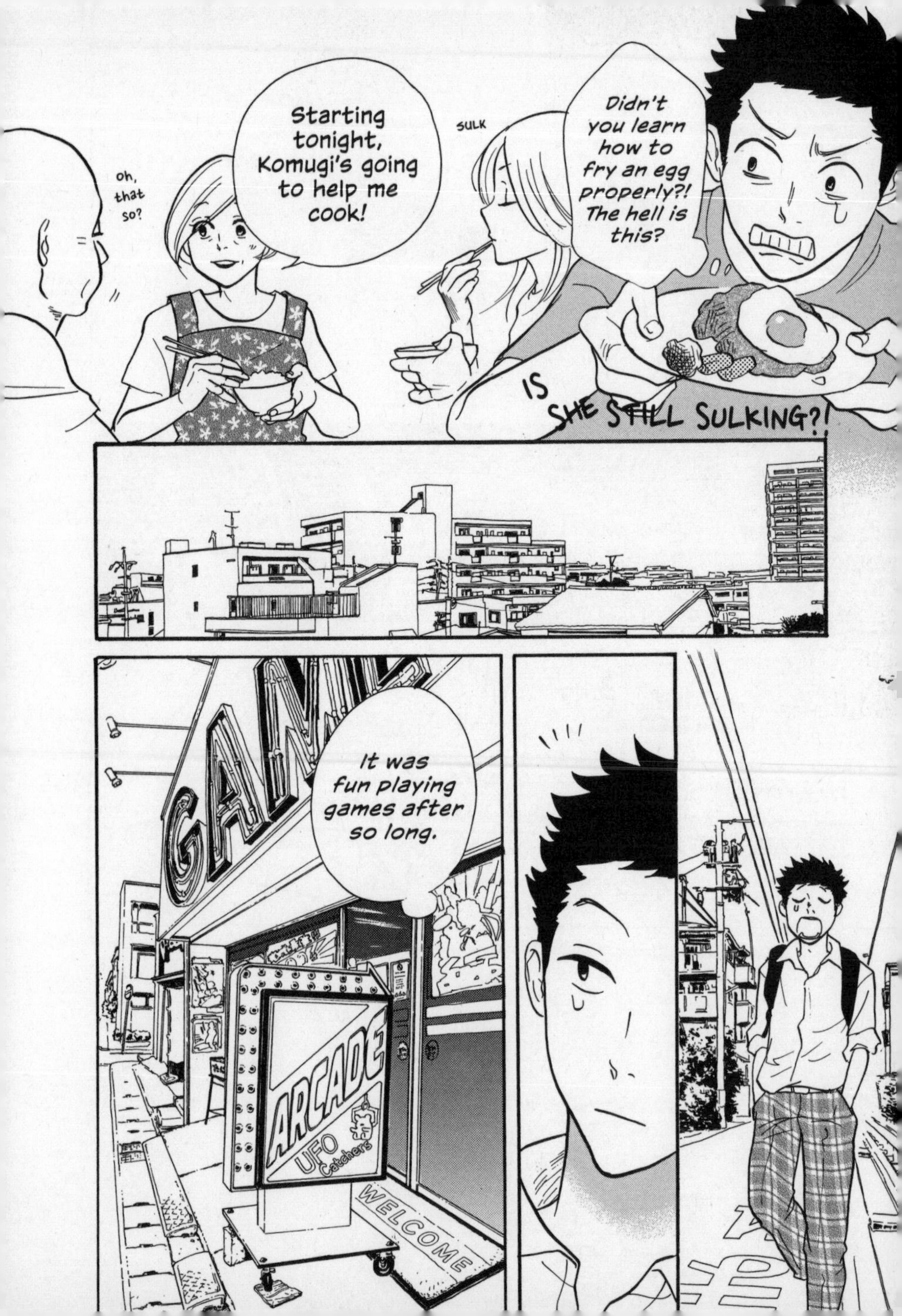
Didn't you learn how to fry an egg properly?! The hell is this?
SULK
Starting tonight, Komugi's going to help me cook!
Oh, that so?
IS SHE STILL SULKING?!
It was fun playing games after so long.
ARCADE
UFO Catchers
WELCOME

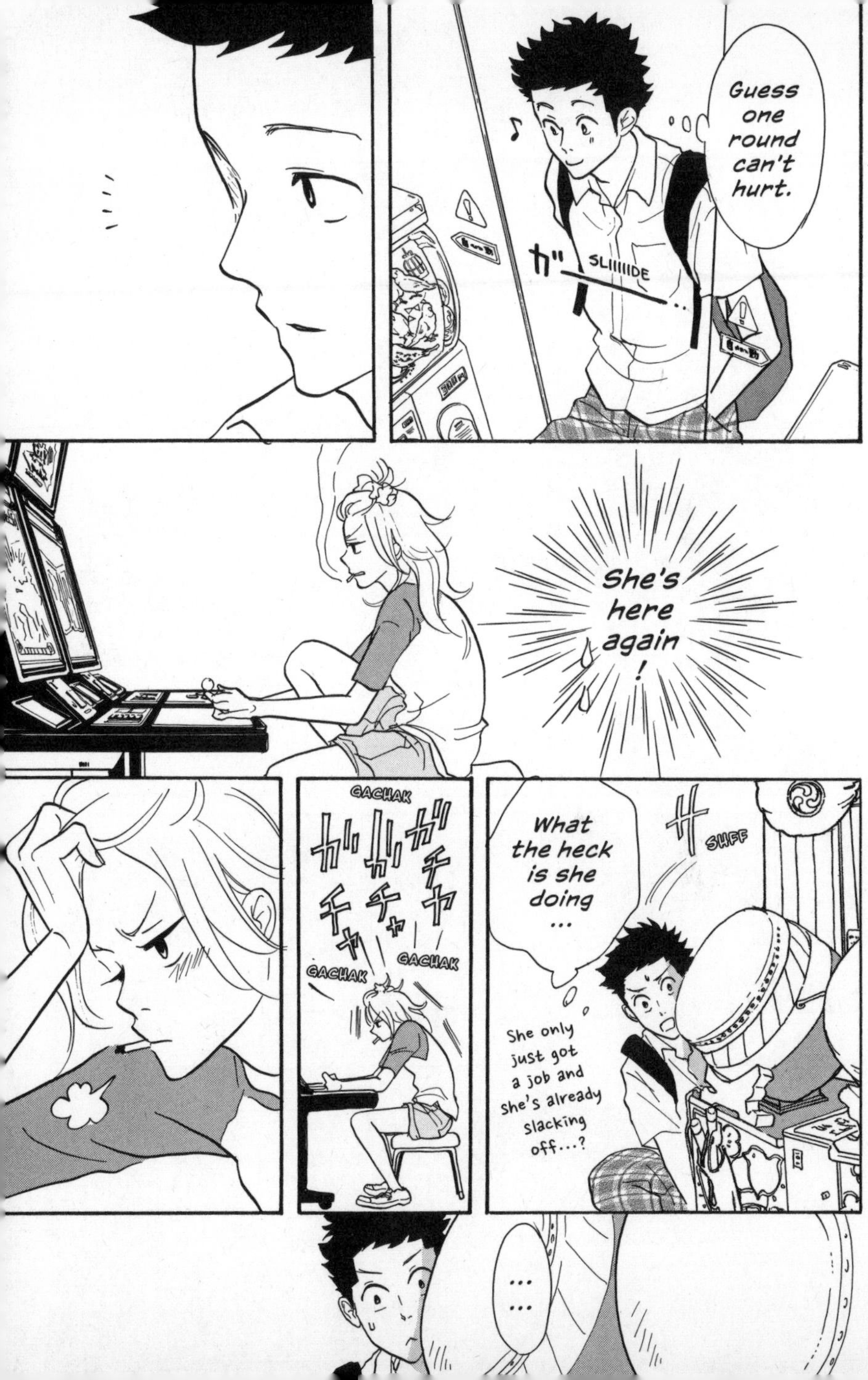
Guess one round can't hurt.
SLIIIIIDE
She's here again!
What the heck is she doing ...
SHFF
She only just got a job and she's already slacking off...?
GACHAK
GACHAK
GACHAK
... ...

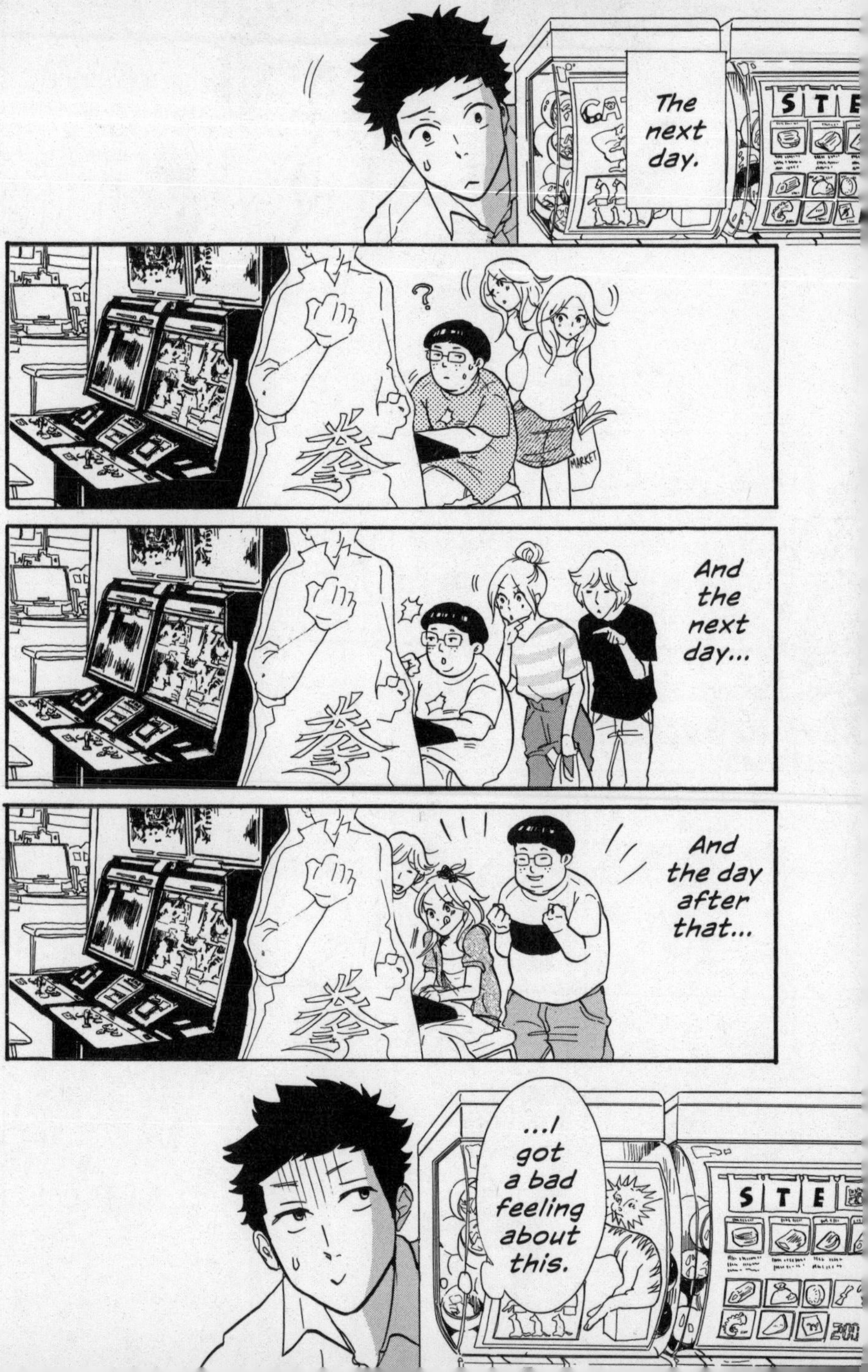

The next day.
And the next day...
And the day after that...
...I got a bad feeling about this.

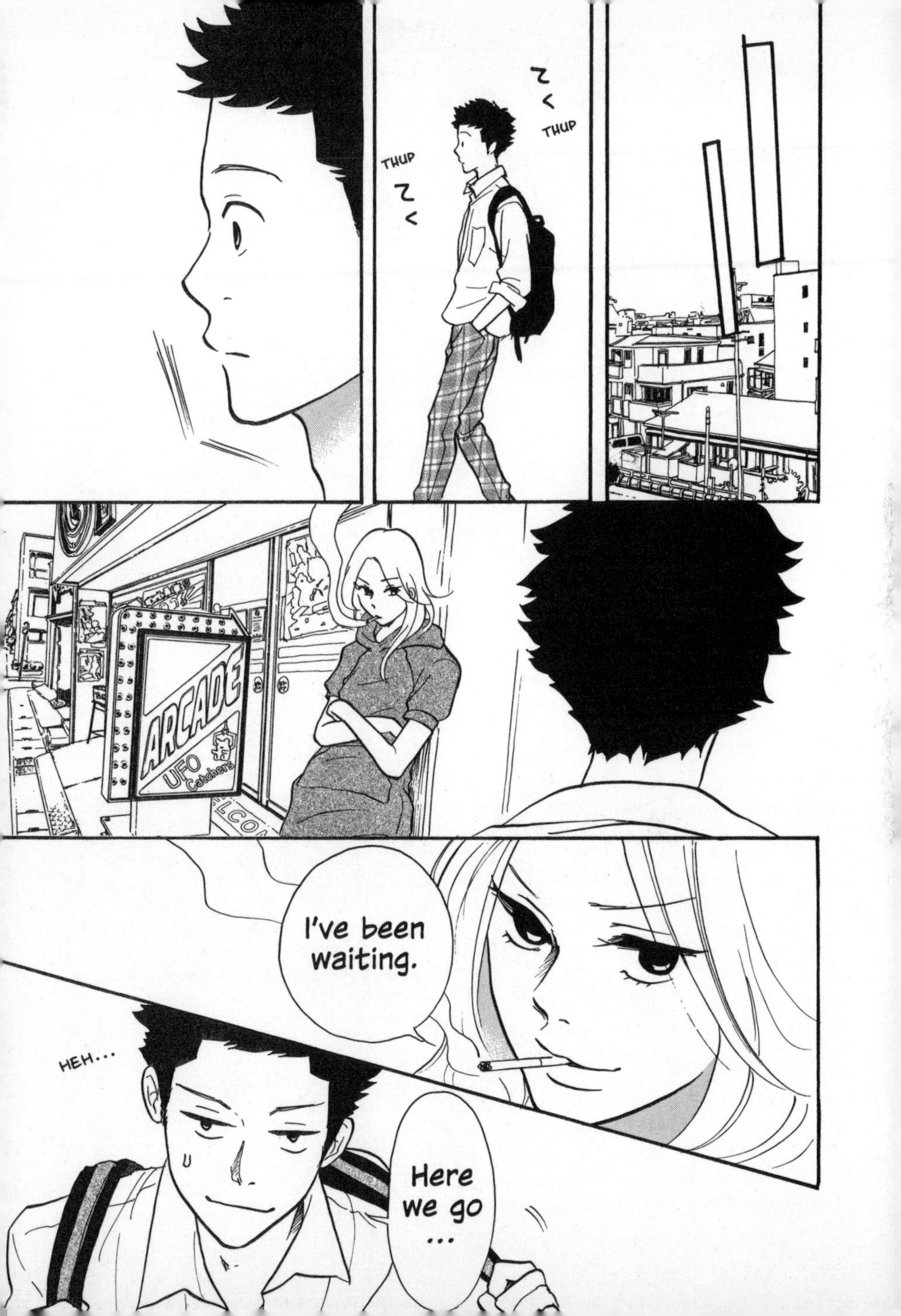
THUP
THUP
ARCADE
UFO Catchers
I've been waiting.
HEH...
Here we go ...

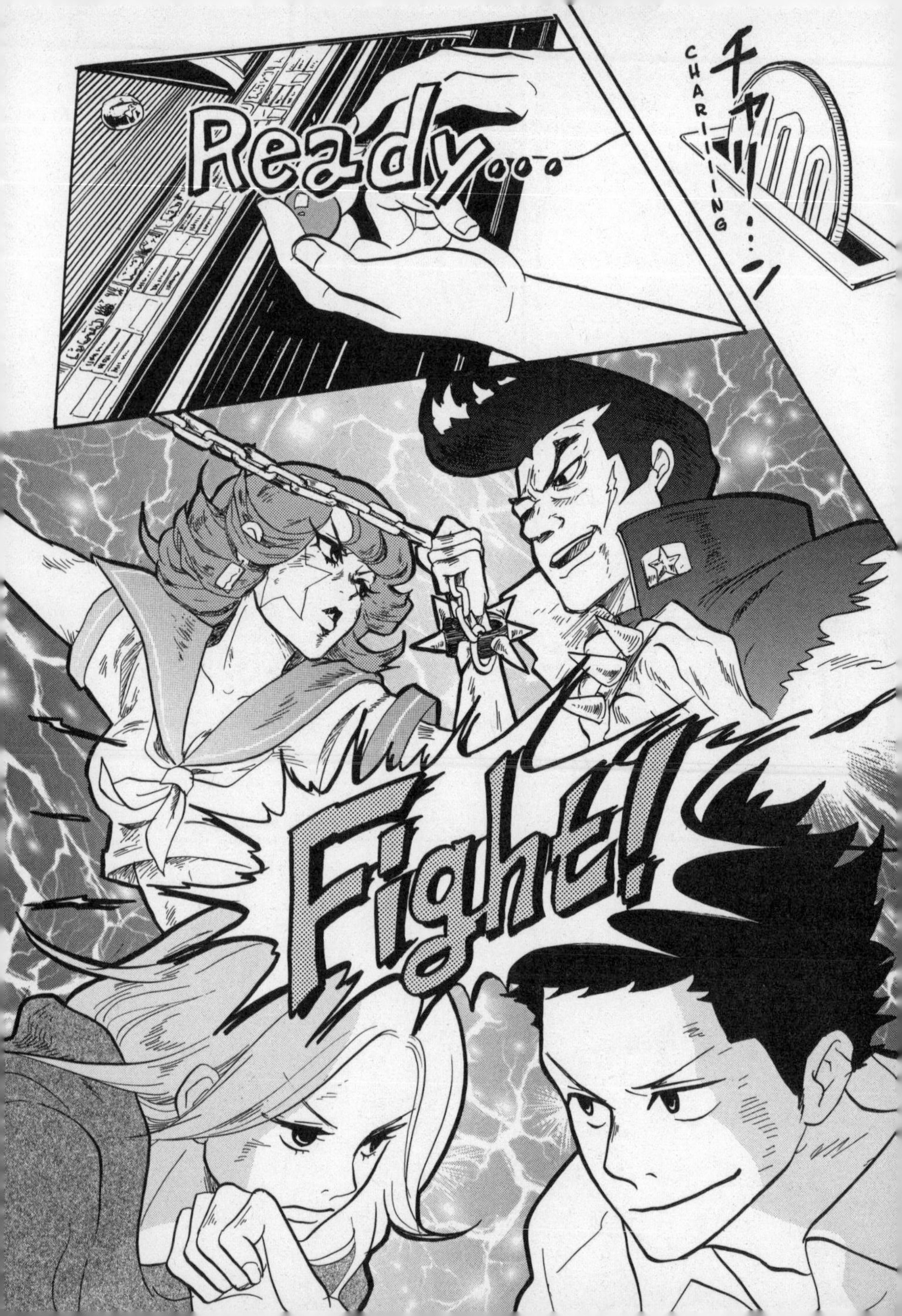
チャリ…ン
CHARIIIING
Ready...
Fight!

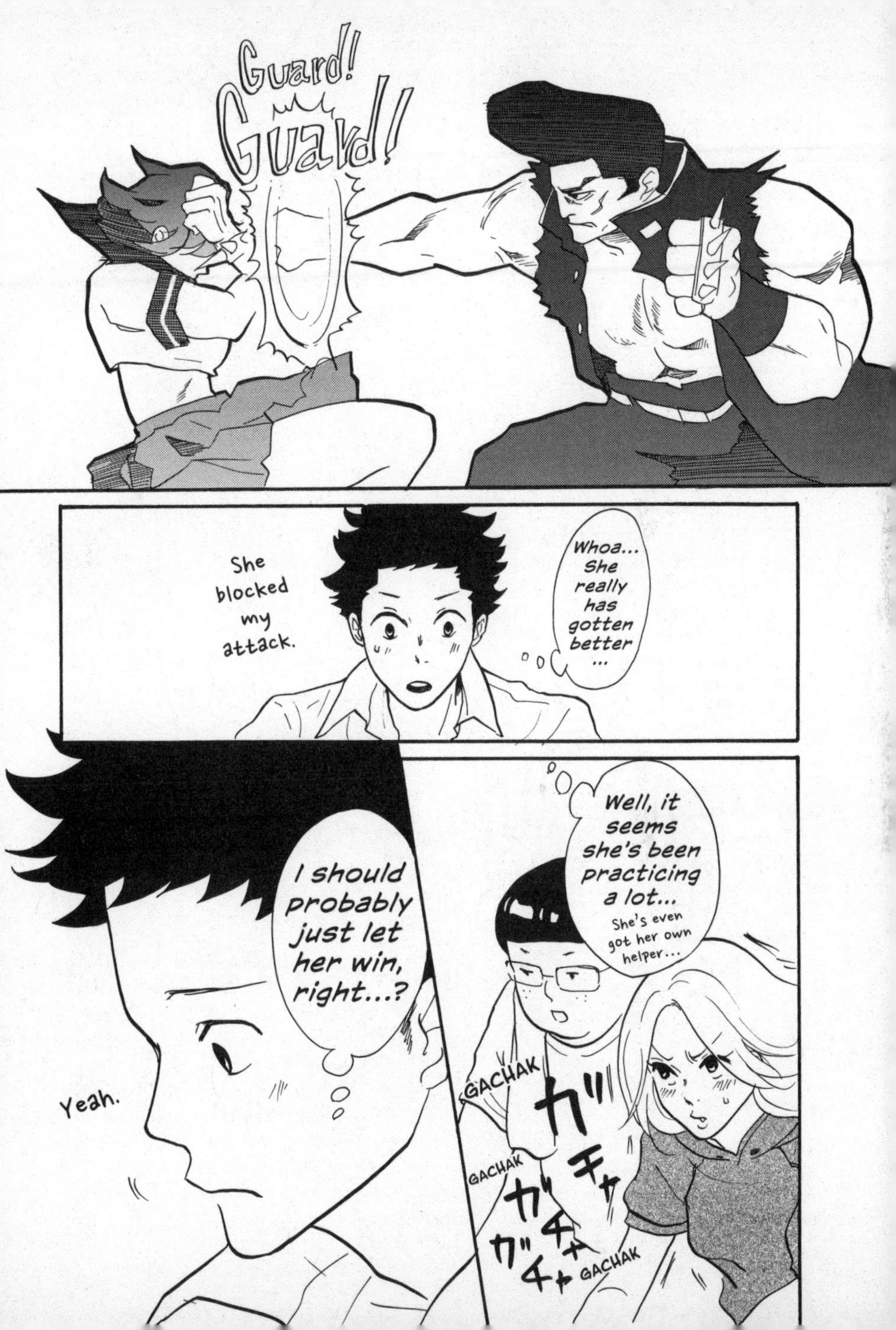
Guard! Guard!
Whoa... She really has gotten better...
She blocked my attack.
Well, it seems she's been practicing a lot...
She's even got her own helper...
GACHAK
GACHAK
GACHAK
I should probably just let her win, right...?
Yeah.

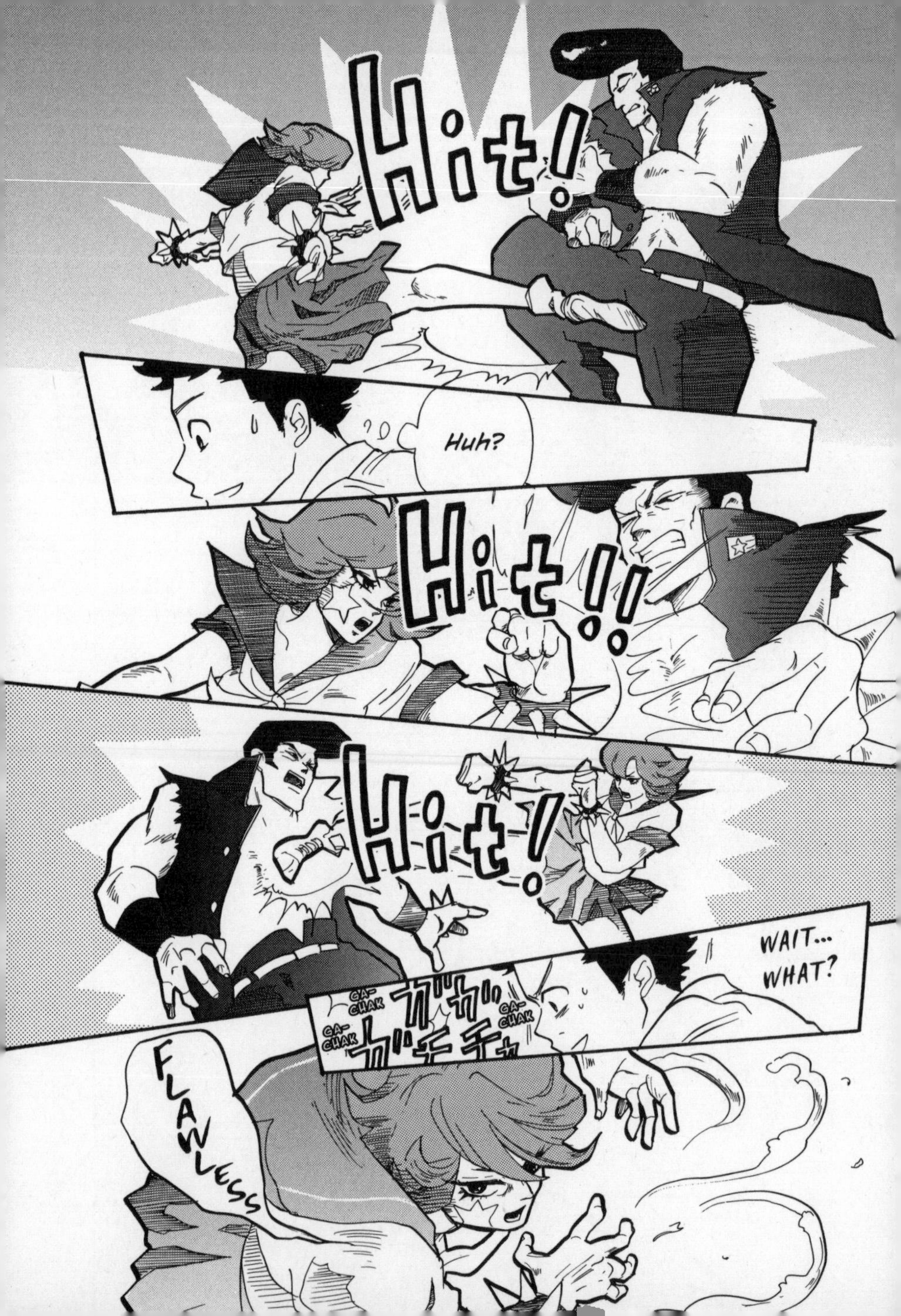
Hit!
Huh?
Hit!!
Hit!
WAIT... WHAT?
GA-CHAK
GA-CHAK
GA-CHAK
FLAWLESS

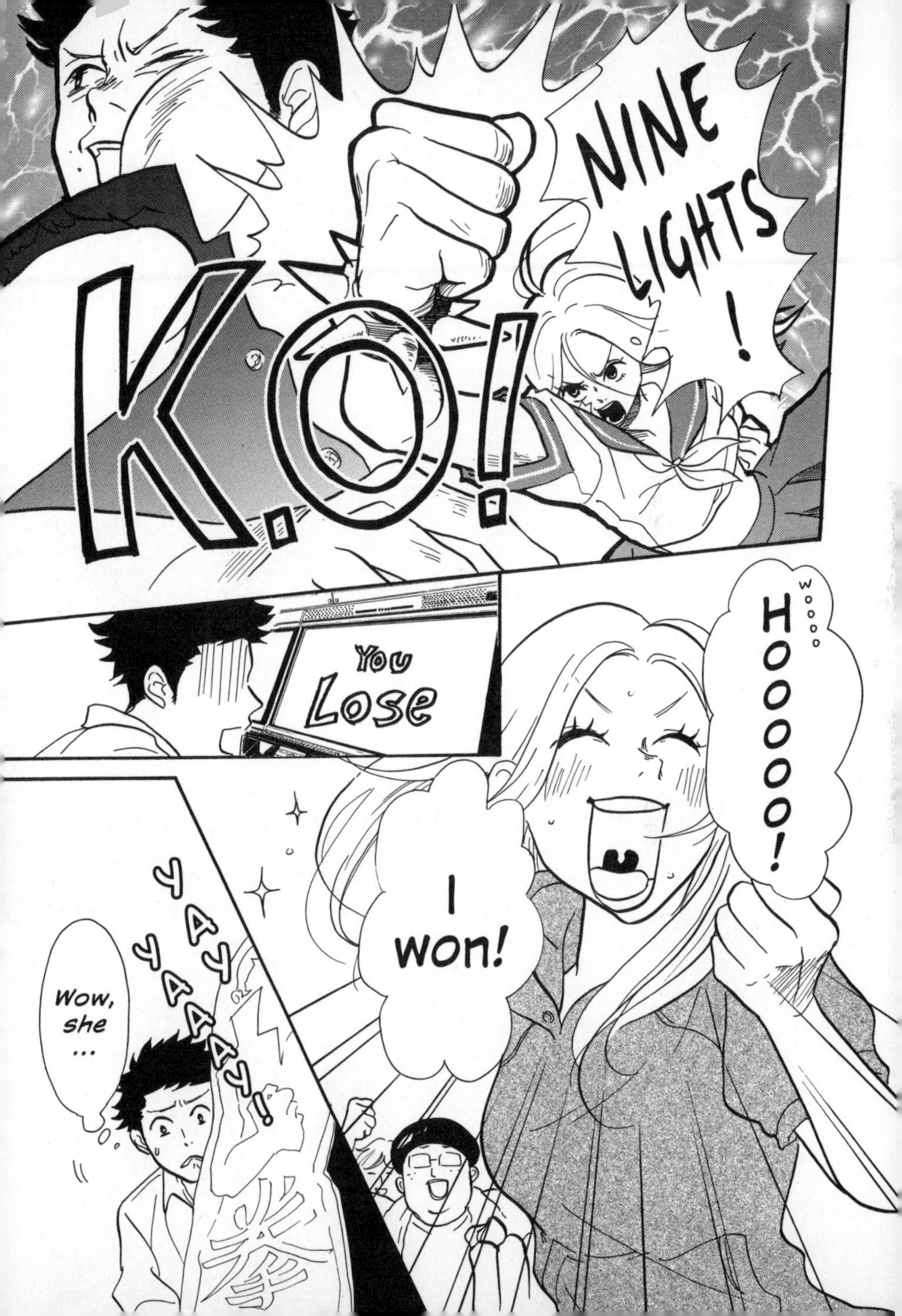
NINE LIGHTS!
K.O.!
WOOOO HOOOOOO!
You Lose
I won!
YAY
YAAAAY!
Wow, she ...

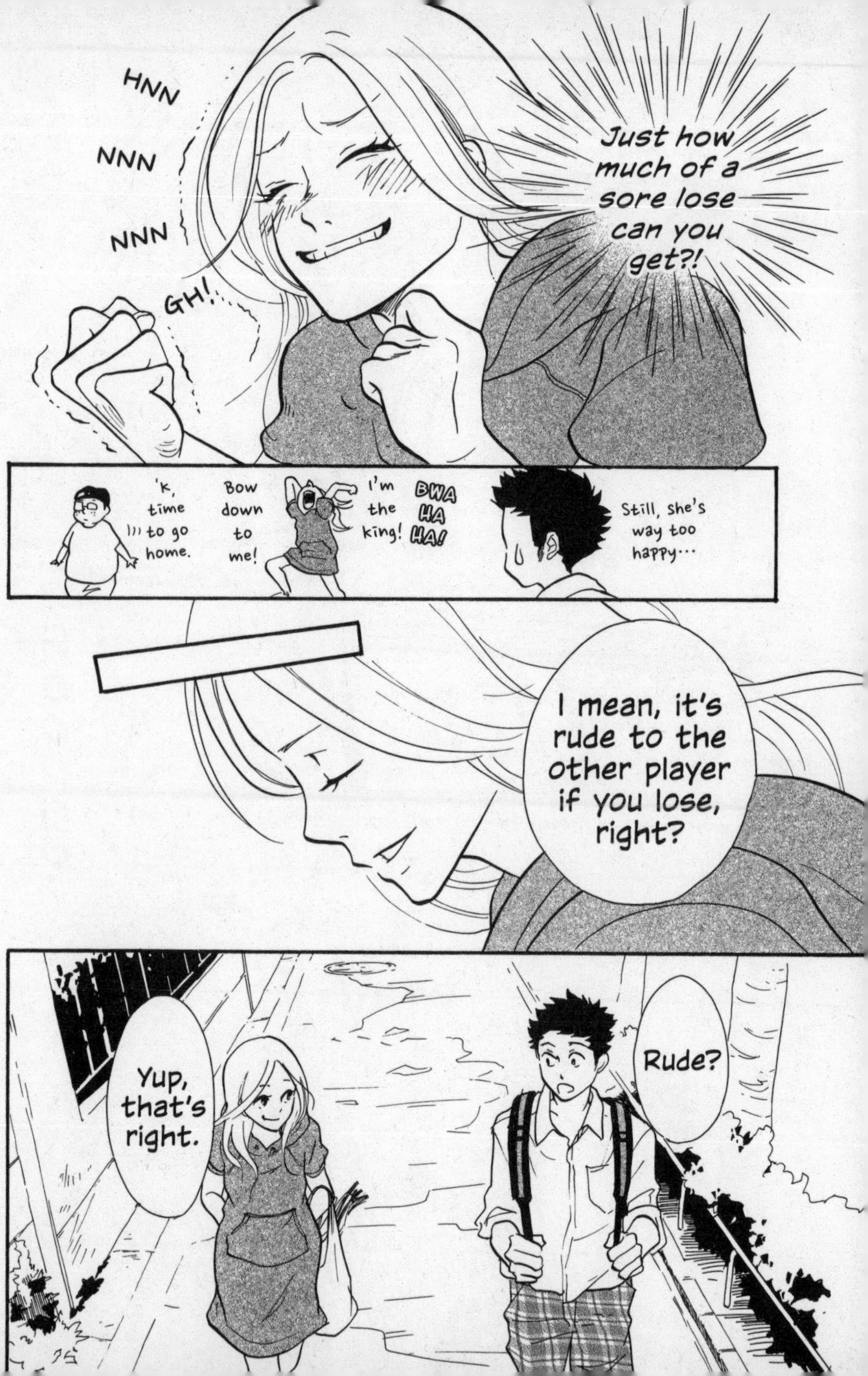
Just how much of a sore lose can you get?!
HNN
NNN
NNN
GH!
Still, she's way too happy...
BWA HA HA!
I'm the king!
Bow down to me!
'k, time to go home.
I mean, it's rude to the other player if you lose, right?
Rude?
Yup, that's right.

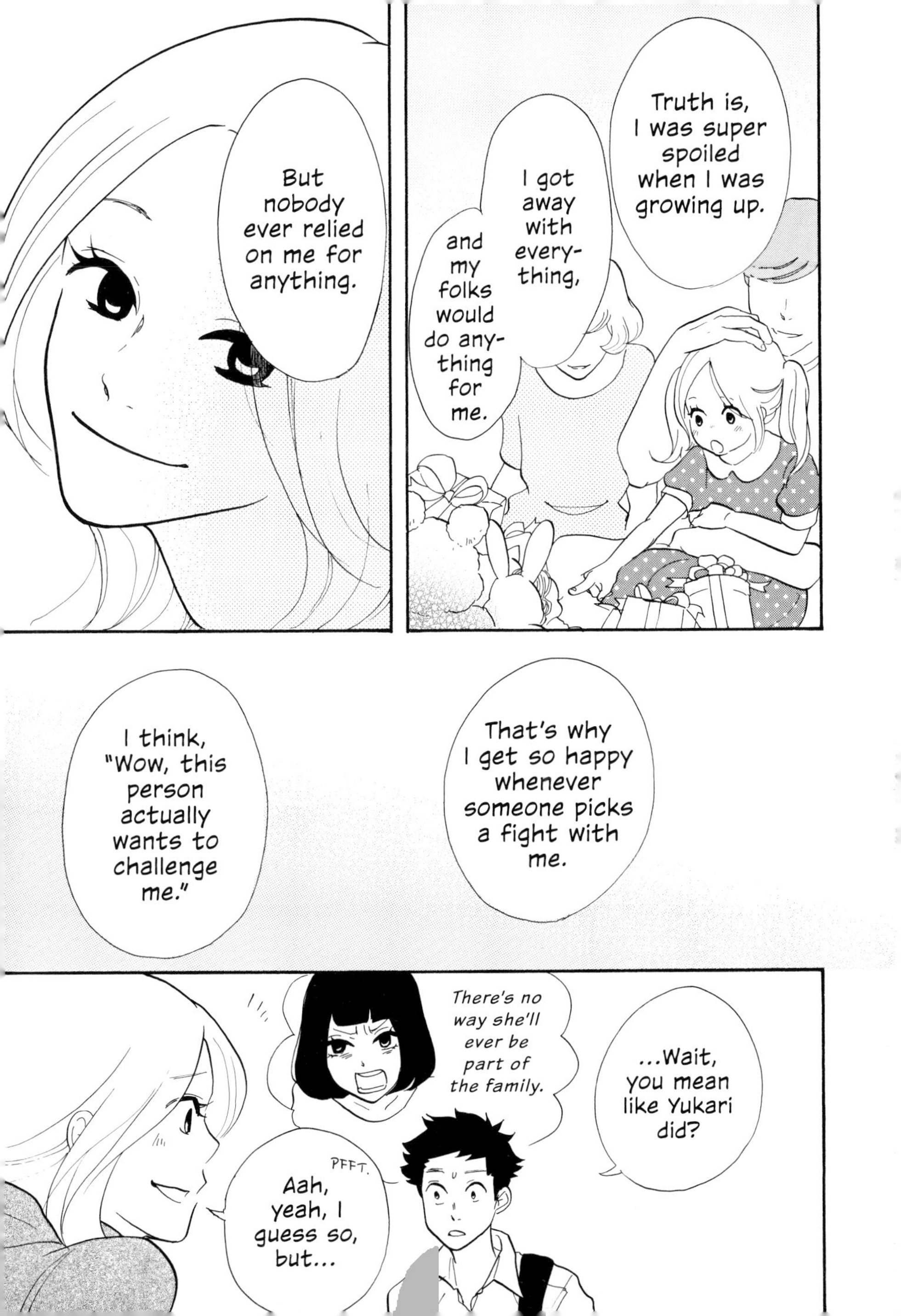
Truth is, I was super spoiled when I was growing up.
I got away with every-thing,
and my folks would do any-thing for me.
But nobody ever relied on me for anything.
That's why I get so happy whenever someone picks a fight with me.
I think, "Wow, this person actually wants to challenge me."
...Wait, you mean like Yukari did?
There's no way she'll ever be part of the family.
PFFT.
Aah, yeah, I guess so, but...

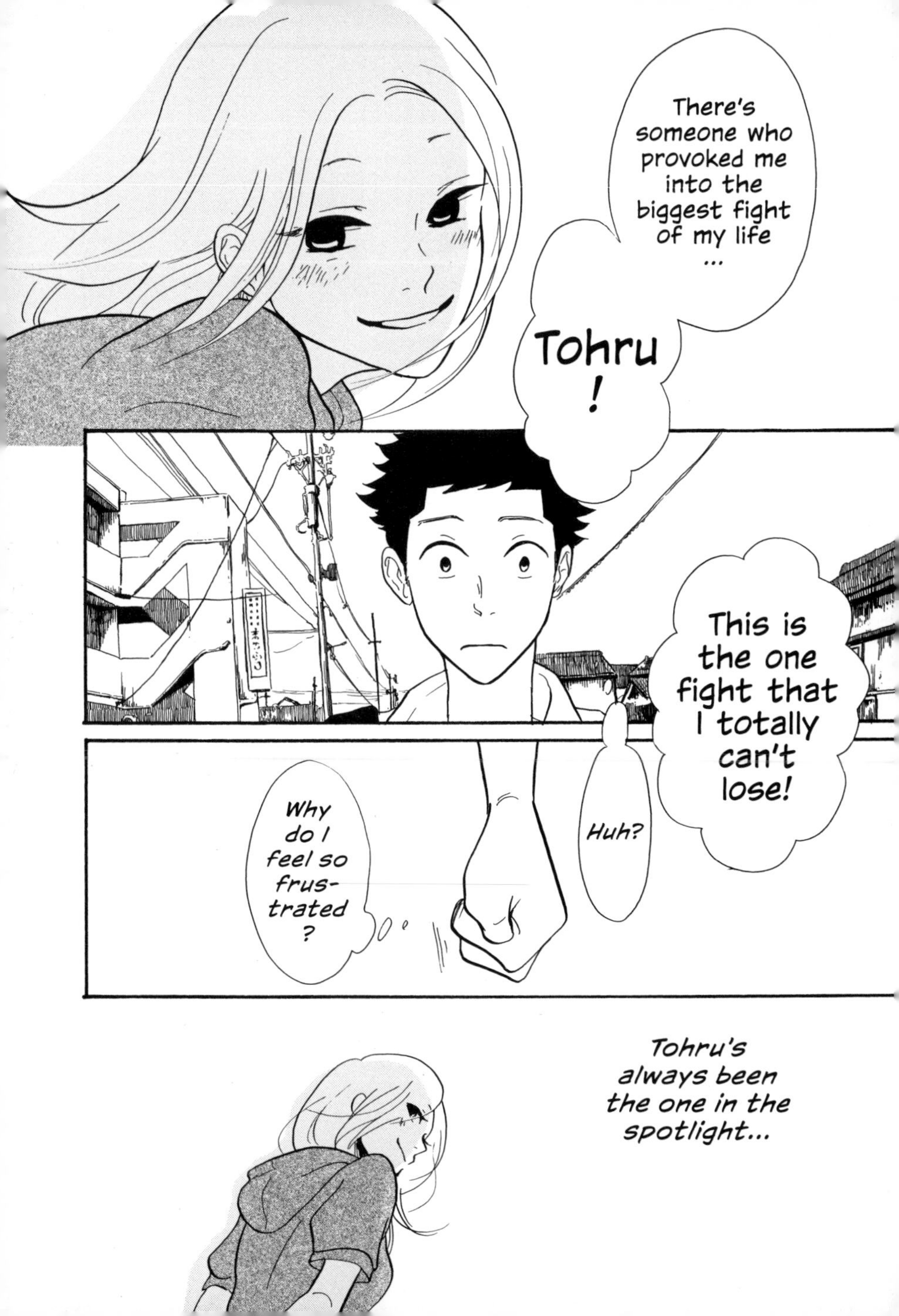
There's someone who provoked me into the biggest fight of my life ...
Tohru!
This is the one fight that I totally can't lose!
Huh?
Why do I feel so frus-trated?
Tohru's always been the one in the spotlight...

12 SISTER-IN-LAW, RIDE HARD!

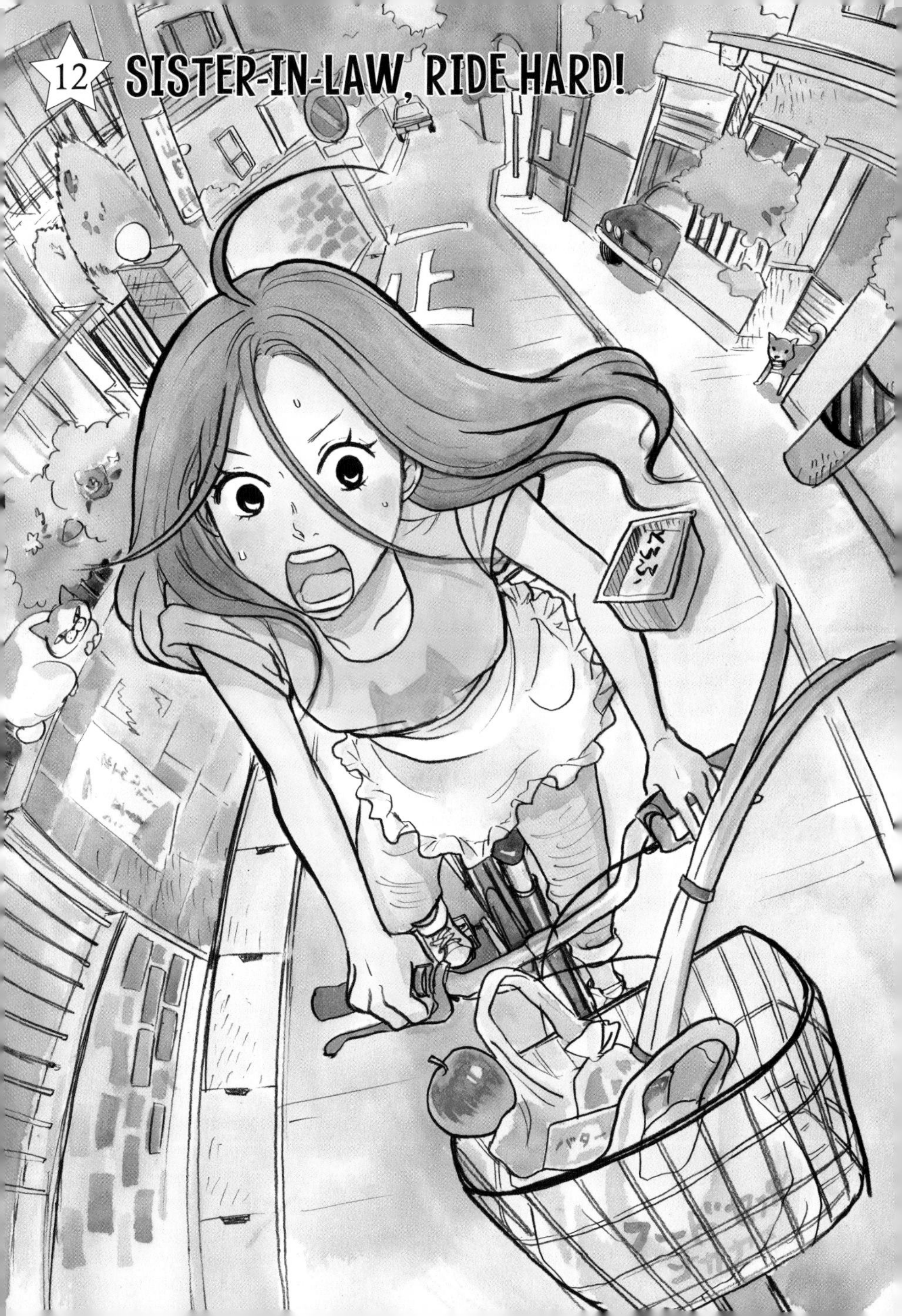

The Delinquent HOUSEWIFE!